WHAT OTHERS ARE SAYING ABOUT THIS BOOK:

A womens divorce lawyer protests: "It is an outrage for this information to be publicized! It will hamstring even the best of us!"

And a womens' protectionist rages: "This book is devastating to the collection process of spousal and child support orders! Absolutely devastating!"

From anonomus: "Jason C. Roberts should have his writings banned from publication, he is destroying the traditional benefits women have rightfully received for many years."

How to Lose Your Ex-Wife Financially Forever!

Escape the Bondage of Excessive Child Support and Alimony

Gain Financial Freedom from Your Ex

JASON C. ROBERTS

SECOND EDITION

LIBERTY BELL PRESS AND PUBLISHING CO.

Salt Lake City, Utah

How to Lose Your Ex-Wife ^ Financially Forever!

JASON C. ROBERTS

Published By:
LIBERTY BELL PRESS AND PUBLISHING CO.
Suite 3-183
4700 South 900 East
Salt Lake City, Utah 84117 U.S.A.

Publishers cataloging in publication data.

ROBERTS, JASON C.
1. "How To Lose Your Ex-Wife (Financially) Forever".
2. "How To" Books.
Library of congress, catalog card number: 90-61343

Printed in the U.S.A.
ISBN 0-922507-05-8 (Softcover)

WHO IS JASON C. ROBERTS ?

Author Jason C. Roberts most certainly ranks as an expert on the subject of preferential treatment offered the female sex in our Civil Divorce Courts. He himself was the victim of a corrupt, and sexually biased court, in the Utah judicial system.

Very quickly, and methodically, the Utah Courts ejected Mr. Roberts from his home, destroying his life as a successful business man, a close and loving father to his five children, and finally, effectively, reduced him to near poverty.

The crippling effects this had on his personal life provided much of the motivation and research for this book.

Mr. Roberts spent almost ten years doing research, and interviewing those, who, like himself, were forced to live on the edge of the law by an uncaring, sexually-biased judicial system.

Mr. Roberts has been a computer engineer and successful restauranteur. This is his second book on the same subject. His first, "Men In The Shadows" was published in 1988.

ACKNOWLEDGMENT

Most authors list on the acknowledgment page almost everyone who may have contributed, no matter how slight, toward the completion of the book.

In my own mind there is only one person who, more that any other, deserves this small, but humble thank you and recognition from a very appreciative new writer.

Over a period of six years, Rosely Barton consistently provided me with the inspiration I needed, along with an ocassional push when my enthusiasm began to wane, to see this project through to completion.

For the numerous mornings she arose at 4:00 AM to work on this manuscript before attending to her own editing career. For her tireless efforts and expertise in editing, proof-reading, correcting, suggesting and word processing. A heart felt thanks to you, Rosely.

Cover by Bill Kuhre

TABLE OF CONTENTS

CHAPTER 1

THE CAUSE OF IT ALL

CHAPTER 2

FINDING THE PERSECUTED MALE

CHAPTER 3

PRE-FADE TECHNIQUES

CHAPTER 4

DURING THE FADE

CHAPTER 5

THE TEMPORARY FADE

CHAPTER 6

THE PARTIAL FADE

CHAPTER 7

THE COMPLETE FADE

THE APPENDICES

WARNING - DISCLAIMER

This book is intended for informational purposes only. No claims or offerings of legal or professional advice are made. If such is desired, please seek competent legal advice.

Neither the author, nor the publisher advocate or condone the violation of Federal, State, or Local laws, and expressly deny suggesting or encouraging the reader to actually use the methods and procedures outlined in this book. Neither do they accept any responsibility or liability for damages resulting from the use of this book's ideas and/or contents.

It is the reader's responsibility to check out and verify all materials in this book for accuracy.

No guarantees, express or implied, are made concerning the information in this book, or the use to which it is put.

WARNING - DISCLAIMER

DEDICATION

This book is dedicated to countless divorced fathers who have displayed unbelievable courage in defying the established procedures of child custody laws by taking their children into a more secure life.

I want to thank those nameless men living in the shadows who confided in me by telling me their stories and ultimately revealing their countless, invaluable, hard-won secrets and procedures.

Jason C Roberts

CHAPTER 1

THE CAUSE OF IT ALL

1. The Overview
2. Child Support
3. Alimony
4. Cases in Point
5. The Fair Property Settlement
6. Pre-Nuptial Agreements

The Overview

The aftermath of divorce can have a variety of meanings for each man involved in this particular type of civil litigation. For some, it is an opportunity for a new life. For others, it may simply be a release from an unpleasant past. But for most, divorce is a relentless, oppressive financial persecution, a never-ending, financial nightmare of alimony and/or excessive child support.

Millions of law-abiding men, finding themselves hopelessly trapped in unjust divorce litigation, have been forced from their homes, separated from their families, and then systematically stripped of their material possessions. All of this is accomplished under the guise of "civil justice", although it smacks more of "jack boots and arm bands".

The Equal Rights movement for women has had little, if any, effect on decreasing the inequable financial burden placed upon the divorced male. A true state of judicial equity for most men still remains but a fantasy. Many men have not only been denied their moral rights as men and fathers, they have been deprived of their civil rights as well. In many cases, they are even denied the freedom to provide for themselves the basic necessities of life.

This book illustrates many of the extreme methods currently used by men to gain freedom from the financial hardships of alimony or excessive child support.

Child Support

Almost every day one hears or reads of the extreme family hardships created by so-called "no-account deadbeats", "thoughtless, irresponsible flakes" living in our society. These are words used to identify the divorced fathers who have deliberately deserted their families and then purposely left their children on the doorstep of poverty. These seemingly endless tales of male inhumanity towards their own offspring have depicted the divorced father as such an incorrigible individual, that all males suffer from this demeaning, undeserved form of "male bashing."

Most are not deserting their children at all! Instead, they are forced underground by excessively punitive laws and made to live "on the edge of the law". All because of the inequities of present divorce laws! The civil courts have made it all but impossible for a divorced father and any future mate to financially live a normal life style. It is a little known but well established fact that the overwhelming majority of divorced fathers who leave their families are compelled to do so out of extreme financial oppression and not from greed or selfish desires.

Most fathers prior to a divorce were probably classified as excellent providers. However, after a divorce breaks the family bonds, the father as a rule is ejected from the household, and financial difficulties for those remaining begin to arise. Is this because the father no longer loves or cares for his children? Absolutely not! The answer lies in the fact that being the rejected member of the family also means a breakdown of authority, and eventually, fatherhood. The rejected father now has only one obligation, and that is to provide financial assistance to children over whom he has no control any more. To divide the income of the father between two households is usually financially devastating, resulting in a degraded lifestyle for all. It is then only a matter of time until a once proud family man will be viewed by his former family as an outsider. A father with no authority, one who is not needed, will eventually lose interest and search for a more meaningful life elsewhere.

Many divorcing males end up losing their home, including all of the furnishings, in addition to having a financially devasting portion of their earnings ear marked for years to come. In addition to the financial losses, they also end up losing their most precious possession of all, the children. If our elected officials really want to stop fathers from fleeing and disappearing forever, they need look no further for the cause of this nation-wide phenomenon than our civil divorce courts! The first step to at least a partial solution is to give <u>automatic, joint physical custody of minor child</u>

ren to both parents. This condition alone will prevent many fathers from seeking a better life elsewhere, under the cloak of anonimity.

To feel needed as a contributing, loved member of the family, and not just an exterior financial source, is absolutely essential. If the woman is given sole custody of the children (as is usually the case), she very often uses this as a weapon against her ex-husband. This usually takes the form of denying the father his visitation rights.

It is a well known, established fact that very few divorcing mothers have the income-producing capabilities of the father; yet civil divorce courts invariably award child custody to the one least able to provide for them, the mother.

Many divorced fathers are compelled to reduce, or even discontinue child support payments altogether because of the waste and corruption practiced by many ex-spouses. Often the child support finances provided by the father are diverted for the mother's personal use, and the children's needs are bypassed. There are countless instances of unethical use of child support payments by a greedy mother, who then blithely ignores the basic requirements of the children. Some women spend well-intended child support on such items as drugs, liquor, tobacco, jewelry, clothing, etc. Some are even supporting a new boy friend out of their child support payments.

When an ex-father objects to this wholesale thievery and attempts to discontinue, or modify his child support payments, he is subjecting himself to contempt of court proceedings and could be jailed for such action. There are numerous cases where a father, tired of seeing his children not receiving the benefits of his labors, has bought for them some of the basic essentials, and then has shortened his check by that amount. This willful altering of his court-ordered child support obligation, again, is considered to be contempt of court! In cases such as this, the well-intended father is not allowed credit for such purchases toward his child support obligation!

It is not an uncommon practice for a vindictive, divorced mother to deny child visitation rights to the father even though he may be paying full child support. Should he, in retribution, attempt to discontinue or modify his child support payments, he can be held in contempt of court. Often, a mother, who has been awarded child custody, will make the children virtually inaccesable to the father by moving hundreds, even thousands of miles away. Even so, he is required to pay full child support for children he cannot see! In these situations no disciplinary action is taken against the mother other than an occasional, minor scolding by a very partial and biased judge.

If a father, without court consent retrives his own children away from the court appointed custodian (the mother), in order to give them a more financially secure life, then our society labels this "kidnapping." If located, the father is treated as a felon in criminal court.

When a woman commits the same action, she is often perceived as justified in exercising her maternal rights!

On a recent episode of 60 Minutes, millions of TV viewers were shocked when a father, originally from a South American nation, disappeared, along with his two small, American-born children and headed back to his native homeland. The producers of the program were very successful in filming the graphic details of the immense sorrow, hurt, and emotional agony that the American mother suffered in her futile attempts to visit them. The mail response was overwhelmingly in favor of the mother's wishes, which was the return of her children. In fact, the most heart-rending aspect was never fully realized by any but a few of the program's viewers. Very few understood that divorced, American fathers by the thousands are subjected to this precise, cruel treatment every day! Only this time, the crime is perpetrated by a mother with court-awarded child custody, and is therefore legal!

Many misunderstood divorced fathers are the unjustified targets of public scorn, ridicule, and discrimination. One of the most blatant forms of unequal treatment lies in our Federal and State Bankruptcy laws. The intent of these laws is to offer the opportunity to begin anew when financial debts are impossible to pay. Unfortunately, most divorced fathers find themselves exempt from these constitutionally-intended provisions.

Any father can make full use of the bankruptcy laws as long as he is married. He can be relieved of certain past-due debts accrued in support of his family such as food, clothing, housing, medical care, etc. However, these privlidges suddenly are no longer available to the divorced father. Because of his divorced status, he is denied full constitutional equality!

If he is unable to continue to pay a crushing amount of child support and/or alimony, he is no longer able to discharge such obligations through bankruptcy.

Even though the Federal Government is responsible for the passage of the bankruptcy act, State Governments have gotten themselves into the picture as well. The various States may enact bankruptcy laws on their own, as long as the Federal laws remain paramount.

The Omnibus Budget Reconciliation Act of 1981 was signed by then President Reagan on August 13 of that year. It is the child support provisions of this law that treat the divorced father as an unequal citizen. The bill states that past due child support amounts can no longer be discharged through bankruptcy as was possible between 1979 and 1981. The Federal law was changed due to a nation-wide campaign by the various State Welfare Agencies, and the lobbying efforts of womens' protectionists groups. These groups erroneously claim that 85 percent of the need nationally supplied by "Aid to Families with Dependent Children" (AFDC) could be eliminated if parents would pay their child support obligations. A correct translation of these new provisions is that since most custodial mothers are incapable of paying their rightful share, this legislation therefore compels the male to pay it for them.

To help resolve the many problems of the financially drowning divorced father, lawmakers must first admit the magnitude of their errors of the past. The very real and terrible crimes that have been commited against the divorced males of this country by State legislators is a national disgrace. Joint physical custody of all minor children between mother and father is absolutely essential! To deny this parental right to the father is an admission by our elected officials that divorced males are not entitled to equality under the law! Since women are clamoring for equal treatment, they should be required to demonstrate their ability to successfully handle their financial future and independence, and prove their ability to provide child support if and when the need arises.

Many women want equality as long as it is simply handed out in the form of a law. But when equal performance and results are required, few are equal to the task. To compel the male partner of a former marriage contract to assume additional financial responsibilities to cover for the inadequacies of an unprepared woman is unacceptable.

Awarding joint physical custody of minor children to both parents must also include equal financial responsibility. The mother must provide complete financial support for the children during her term of custody, the same way the father would while the children were living with him. To legally accept and excuse a woman's inability to financially provide for herself and her children as is required of the father, only demonstrates the lack of equality now practiced. Many readers will cry "foul" at being exposed to these new ideas, but if women truly want to feel equal to men, they will see the justice and wisdom involved. It will only be the woman with a parasitic nature who will disapprove.

Most courts and lawmakers claim to have the wellbeing of the children in mind when rendering a decision or making a new law that affects them. The present-day divorce and child custody laws are a complete failure. Ask any child from a broken home if he or she likes for Mom to be in sole charge and living exclusively with her, and only visiting with Dad on occassions. The answer is usually an overwhelming "no". Practically all children from divorced homes relish the prospect of living half of the time with their father.

Excessive child support obligations are an evil of our society, and have no place in a land of free men. This highly discriminatory practice is sexist in nature as it applies almost exclusively to men, for very few women pay any form of child support to the father of their children. Child support should be considered excessive in all situations where the divorced father is compelled to pay higher amounts than he is capable of paying, while still maintaining a reasonably adequate life style for himself.

These situations are invaribly created by divorced women who have no marketable job skills and cannot earn an adequate income to provide for herself, much less provide her rightful share of child support. The elected lawmakers' imbecilic solution to the problem is to give custody to the woman, who is least capable of providing the financial support, and place the excessive financial burden directly on the shoulders of the father.

That these incredibly unjust and discriminatory laws against males were passed in the first place, and then were able to survive in the judicial system as we know it today surely demonstrates the incompetence of our lawmakers! Why the United States Superme Court has not struck down these obviously unconstitutional practices of male discrimination is not only incredible, but unconscionable!

Now is the time for divorced men nation-wide to unite and stand together. Not in small, isolated groups and pockets as we see today, but as a united, national orginization with substantial voting power. Only then will State and Federal lawmakers recognize this as a threat to their precious careers, and pass the legislation neessary to correct these unjust evils.

Practically all of the damaging charges aimed at destroying the divorced father go unanswered and unchallenged in the media. The divorced fathers of this country badly need a national organization coupled with articulate, informed spokesmen to reply to the thousands of false charges and statements presently circulated.

For years, undeserving, non-achieving women have been busy lobbying State and Federal lawmakers that mothers by nature are the rightful and logical heir-apparent to the children once a marriage breaks up. The father's primary, and sometimes only right, is to provide financial support for the mother and children. Women have been extremely successful in getting these highly discriminatory laws passed which are in effect today.

Since men represent the vast and overwhelming majority of this nation's responsible, full-time, life-long wage earners both in Government and Commerce, it is logical to assume that they should want to protect themselves from the unfair treatment heaped on them by our courts. This however is not true as exemplified by the divorce laws presently on the books. It is only after a man goes though a divorce and/or child custody litigation himself that he realizes the gross inequities involved.

The USA is often boastingly referred to as, "The Land of the Free." Pity the uninformed who expound such notions! Chances are, they have never undergone the tribulations of a civil divorce and experienced the loss of family and financial freedom! To many divorced males, these statements sound hollow and meaningless for they do not apply equally to all.

Alimony

In less-than-diplomatic terms, alimony could be described as the "Bastard" child of extortion, or "Spousal Blackmail". The concept of alimony should shrivel the very soul of decent, freedom-respecting individuals! To enslave one human being to another in financial bondage simply because the marriage partnership has been dissolved is judicial insanity. Since only men (with rare exceptions) pay this form of extortion, it should be listed as yet another prime example of male discrimination in our society.

One man bitterely stated that whoever fosters or condones the precepts of alimony should be rejected from the human race and reclassified as "pond scum".

The word alimony has such a bitter connotation that Social Services bureaucrats have futilely attempted to soften the term to "spousal support." However, the newly-manufactured title has not gained the hoped-for, public acceptance, for regardless of the term applied, it still constitutes one of the more ugly forms of male degradation.

No human being should so degrade him or herself as to accept such undeserved monetary support earned by others.

Alimony, like excessive child support, is condoned and supported mainly by women's protectionists. These groups are organized for the benefit of the non-achieving woman who is unable or unwilling to provide for herself and her children the essentials of life. These female under-achievers, since their number is legions, are also highly supported by elected legislators and, of course, tax-supported bureaucrats. These officials desperately want her off the welfare rolls, and have conveniently placed the financial burden on the ex-husband. Since women are demanding equality in the business world, they should be willing to accept equal responsibility when the marriage contract comes to an end.

Our lawmakers have created the monster called alimony with its attendent hideous stench and have imposed its cruelty mainly on the male sex. Practically all States have the legislated power to impose fines, and/or imprisonment for those men who fail to pay. This, in spite of the fact that debtors' prison in the Unites States has been unconstitutional for ages! To conveniently bypass the constitutionality issue, the charge has been neatly altered to contempt of court. Do lawmakers ever really wonder why the credibility of the judicial system has slipped to such a low ebb? Regardless of the devious side-stepping maneuver used in prosecuting alimony violators, the bottom line is still debtors' prison. No man should be compelled to pay alimony of any amount, and is fully justified to join those men in the shadows, as a matter of moral principle.

Cases In Point

Consider the conversation that took place on February 2, 1981. The incident involved Mrs. Karolyn Rose, (ex-wife of former baseball super star, Pete Rose), and Gary Collins, on an afternoon television talk show. Karolyn Rose started the conversation by crudely relating to the audience the large sum of money owed her by ex-husband Pete as a result of a recent divorce settlement. Mr. Collins attempted to discreetly get off the sensitive subject by starting to talk of baseball. He asked what made Pete such a hard-working, dedicated player and fierce competitor? Karolyn, obviously not willing to change the subject, replied, "I worked hard too, getting all that money from him." Gary Collins, now desperate to get back to baseball, asked, what made Pete play so hard in the playoff series against the Phillies? "He's a freak", replied Karolyn, "he plays hard because he owes me so much money he has to play hard".

This attitude of disdain and contempt toward the male who previously provided her with much more than merely the essentials of life is typical of non-achieving women. Our divorce laws have created a leverage and sanctuary that many divorced women use to hide behind in order to financially subdue and/or destroy an ex-husband.

The actual settlement itself, as expected, was a travesty of justice slanted toward the undeserving. Pete got to keep his 1979 Porche. Karolyn was awarded a 1978 Rolls Royce. She also got the $300,000 house, while Pete got to keep the $175,000 house. Karolyn also got a 1978 jeep, all personal and household effects, plus a whopping $1.2 million in alimony, plus $3000 per month in child support. Of course, Karolyn got custody of the Roses' two children, Fawn, then 16, and Pete Jr., then 11. Last, but not least, Pete was given the dubious honor of keeping his own, hard-earned athletic trophies!

The obvious question on the Pete Rose divorce settlement should be, just what did Karolyn Rose actually contribute to the marriage to justify the financial returns she eventually received? Did she have an income of any type which contributed to the finances during the marriage? Did she invest in the countless thousands of hours necessary to develop an athletic body, and the required physical skills? Did she ever take her turn in the batting lineup to face a ninety-mile-an-hour fast ball? Did she ever experience the pain, bumps, bruises, broken bones and other injuries suffered by most professional baseball players? If the answer to these questions is no, as we know it is, could we then venture the statement that Karolyn Rose surely must be one of the world's highest paid baby sitters?

The divorce settlement between TV star Johnny Carson and his ex-wife Joanna has been widely publicized in the television media, as well as in print. Johnny himself makes continuous references to "what used to be mine" on his own late night TV talk show. Even though these "jokes" are perceived by millions of viewers in a humorous vein, it is in fact, a human tragedy.

Joanna, the consuming, non-providing member of the now-defunct marrage received a luxurious Bel Air mansion with all of its furniture and furnishings valued at more then $3 million; three New York apartments complete with all furniture and furnishings, estimated value, $3 million; the sum of $5 million in cash plus $35,000 per month in alimony for 64 months; a 50% share of Johnny's future pensions, valued at more than $4 million; a half-interest in residuals on Johnny's 1972-82 shows; all of the jewelry and personal effects she acquired during the marriage; one half of the stock in Vollbracht Design, a firm that provides outfits for the stars, including Joan Rivers; one half of Johnnys interest in the Albuquerque Broadcasting Co, plus at least half of Johnnys interest in nine other companies; a Rolls Royce with the license plate IJANDJ, a Mercedes-Benz with the license plate 1BABES, and an additional 1981 Datsun; several works of art including a Picasso, 310 shares of Carson Broadcasting Co., and last, but not least, 75 Krugerrands.

Could one say that Joanna displayed indescribable greed, coupled with incredible gall, when she later appealed the alimony sum, claiming it was too small for her to live on? Fortunately, the presiding judge did not allow an increase in the alimony amount and Joanna was forced to exist on the meager amount previously alloted.

This partial breakdown of the divorce settlement should convince even the most liberal of constitutional students that our civil laws concerning divorce litigation have been badly infected by so-called "woman protectionism." To fall back on those tired, old, worn-out, overly-used statements that these settlements are justified because the male involved can afford it, does not in any way create justification! There are no moral grounds for such a complete disregard for the principles of fair play as prescribed by the Founding Fathers in writing our constitution. To bestow such grossly favorable, unearned rewards on a particular and non-achieving segment of our population simply because of sex, is inexcusable. To say that our State Legislators have unleashed an "AIDS" type virus aimed at the destruction of the principles of judicial equality is a gross understatement.

The two previous case histories involved the rich and famous. What about the ordinary guy? How does he fare in normal divorce litigation? Unfortunatly, the average male emerges from divorce court in considerably worse shape than the affluent because of his severely reduced financial capabilities. The average male is often unable to continue supporting his own personal needs in a reasonable manner, especially if he has two or more children on his court-ordered child support obligation.

As an illustration of exactly how far our society has adapted itself toward women protectionism, let's look at the case of Linda and Steve (not their real names). Both had been previously married when they met. Steve entered this new marriage childless, Linda had two teenage daughters by her first husband. She was of course successful in getting legal custody of the children from her first discarded husband who by now was forgotten. She was delighted to move into Steve's home, along with her two daughters.

Over the ensuing years Steve maintained a long history as an excellent provider and husband to Linda, and step father to her girls. He successfully reared both daughters to maturity, and helped them in turn to have successful marriages of their own. The family was so close that he eventually became accepted as their real father.

The steel mill where Steve worked suddenly closed after almost seventy years of operation. Steve was getting close to retirement, and for the first time in his life found himself unemployed. After several months of financial hardship, Linda was forced to go to work. After more than a year of unemployment, Steve still found himself unable to find work. Linda was distraught over their financial situation and filed for divorce.

As in most of these situations, the male member was shown no gratitude for his valiant efforts of the past. Instead, he was systematically reduced to poverty. Linda felt totally justified in taking 50% of virtually everything her husband had worked for. She received one half of the equity in his house, most of the furnishings, one of the family cars, all of the savings account, and half of any retirement Steve would receive in the future.

The unjust rationale here is obvious to all except lawmakers. In actuality, Steve played the role of father and good samaritan in providing a home and all of the requirements of life for Linda and her daughters. In most parts of the world, Steve's actions would have been considered generous, compassionate, and kind-hearted. Under those circumstances, Linda might have displayed heartfelt appreciation and gratitude. Even though Steve was honorable and provided for Linda and her daughters in their time of need, Linda, in turn, did not feel so inclined when Steve became needy.

These erroneous and hurtful ideals, long accepted by many women in our society, have been fostered and enlarged over the years by tradition. The time of "women protectionism" must be phased out, and the laws which uphold these antiquated ideals must be written off the books now.

The Fair Property Settlement

When a man and a woman are in the process of dissolving their marriage, the divorce should be treated the same way as when business partners end their business agreement, namely, they are in the process of liquidating stock and closing the doors! Fair play and equal justice must apply to both partners. To offer any type of advantage to a particular partner based on sex should not be permissible. The first rule to apply should be the automatic return of all property to the rightful owner obtained prior to the marriage agreement. The property obtained after the marriage agreement should be returned to the individual who actually provided the finances for such property. This is the area where woman protectionism emerges, and the unjust advantage is applied in her favor every time. Community property laws were contrived mainly to provide women protectionism.

If the woman was employed for a portion of the marriage, she should rightfully be entitled to a fair return on her investment. As an example, if she provided 40% of the income during the term of the marriage, then she should be rightfully entitled to 40% of the assets in the property settlement.

However, if the woman was not employed, had no financial income, and did not contribute financially, she should be entitled to absolutely nothing in the property settlement. These statements may be considered shocking and unorthadox by women protectionists, but their value and justification are obvious.

The pressing question in the womens protectionist's mind is, what about the time and efforts spent by the woman in such functions as wife, mother, homemaker, etc. Some publications have gone so far as to categorize the talents and efforts of the married woman, even assigning monetary value to the various tasks performed. In addition to having been wife and mother, these publications generally include such dubious occupations as sex partner, accountant, cook, launderss, seamstress, chauffeur, gardener, teacher etc., etc., the list goes on and on. A dollar value is usually calculated by estimating the time spent in each function. This final, often highly exaggerated figure is then submitted as the "true worth" of a woman's contribution toward the marriage.

What the womens protectionist deliberatly fails to include on the financial statement is the actual monetary expenses incurred by the husband in keeping a wife, more commonly known as overhead. Or, as the business man would say, the cost of doing business. If the married man should compute the actual costs of supporting a wife, he could generate a list of his own. These overhead expences could include her meals, snacks, candy, eating out, clothing, cleaning, her share of the rent and utilities, medical, and dental expences, gifts such as jewlery, hair care, cosmetics, beauty aids, credit cards, allowance, social fees, lessons of all types, club dues, insurance premiums, vacations, car expences etc., etc.

All of these expenses a single woman has to provide for herself, but in the case of the non-working, married women, are provided by her husband. If the husband's actual overhead costs are subtracted from the woman's calculated "true worth" figure it would no doubt show that she was very well paid for any services rendered. In fact, most non-working women would likely end up in debt to their husband! The amount the male spends on just keeping a wife would more than compensate her for her time and effort. Why then, should the divorcing woman be entitled to an additional portion of any property accumulated during the marriage, if she did not contribute financially? The reasoning is obvious, it is the discriminatory intent of the female protectionist.

Pre-Nuptial Agreements

If the divorced male should ever consider another marriage, especially in a community property state, he must protect his assets. One of the prime uses for pre-marital agreements is for couples who have been married before and who have accumulated substantial assets. The agreement not only ensures that a spouse won't get any part of those assets in the event of divorce, but the assets will go to whom designated by either party.

It is essential that a qualified attorney draw up the agreement in the event that it is challanged in court. If future earnings are to be protected, it must be worded carefully and legally by a professional. Taking the risk to write one independently is foolish, because defending it in court could prove difficult and expensive.

CHAPTER 2

FINDING THE PERSECUTED MALE

1. The Overview
2. Who Will Be In Pursuit?
3. Methods Of Location
4. Interpretations
5. The Statute Of Limitations
6. Some Good Advice

The Overview

How many persecuted males are wanted for past due child support, and/or alimony? The figures vary widely depending on who publishes the report. The exact number is of course unknown, but is estimated to be around ten million. Of this amount, an overwhelming percentage of men would like to escape from an ex-wife forever, and some actually do. Most however lack the knowledge to effectively disappear for any appreciable length of time. Of the divorced males who eventually decide to become inaccessible mainly for financial reasons, a large number is found within several years, only to face additional financial litigation. Some end up sentenced to prison.

However, those armed with the necessary knowledge and procedures often successfully vanish into a new and totally different lifestyle. The law of preservation and survival compells many of these men to fade into another identity, with the hoped-for possibility to again know peace of mind. Divorced men sought because of child support or alimony are referred to in this book as, "Persecuted Males." Those who have successfully vanished and entered a fade, are known as "Men in the Shadows."

Who Will Be In Pursuit?

Once a man is suspected of living in the shadows, the adversary will consist of a formidable army of extremely capable and well-heeled individuals. To underestimate their talents and resources would be foolhardy, because they are liberally supported by State and Federal tax dollars. Their main function in life is to seek out, expose, and financially destroy the a once admired family man.

Just who are these unseen enemies? The pursuers, as they are often referred to, are identified as the nation's "Welfare Agency Bureaucrats", and associated investigative Agencies, such as "The Department of Recovery Services" also known as "Social Services Investigators." Some States may have different titles for their own Agency, but the goal is a common one: the apprehension and financial destruction of those men owing past due child support and/or alimony.

These tax supported bureaucrats are guilty of squandering millions of tax dollars to persecute one segment of the population, the divorced male. This is part of the same tax consuming fraternity that depletes tax revenues on the undeserving such as the lazy, criminal rehabilitation programs, those lost souls in the drug culture, and women without marketable job skills. How many other derelicts from society reside on the welfare rolls one can only guess.

And so, the financially burdened, divorced male, is often forced underground in order to protect what few assets he still has.

The Social Services investigator is usually prompted into action as a result of a written complaint filed by an ex-wife who has not received her full child support or alimony payments. This action may also be initiated by the Social Services Recovery Department if the woman is on welfare. Even though these organizations are primarily controlled by State Government, they have full cooperation and receive additional funding and parental tracking information (usually men only) from several Federal Agencies, including, among others, the Department of Health, Education and Welfare (HEW), the Department of Internal Revenue (IRS), the Department of Social Security, and the US Military with all of its branches.

The Social Services investigator can utilize a full bag of tricks including deception, in order to extract the information needed when tracing missing husbands. He may resort to assuming a false identity, if this will aid the cause.

In a recently reported case, a man living in the shadows was located after almost nine years of peaceful anonymity. His sister, who had faithfully served as his contact, was duped by a clever investigator into revealing his whereabouts. The investigator in question cleverly portrayed himself as an insurance representive from the Veterans Administration, St. Paul, Minnesota. He falsely reported to the unsuspecting and devoted but gullible sister that her brother's G.I. insurance policy had matured and was to pay a one-time dividend of $9,000.00. However, unless claimed within ten days, the entire amount would be forfeited and lost.

The investigator inferred that his office had tried in vain for years to locate the recipient of this dividend.

Social Services

State of Utah
Executive Director

This is an example of how some state's Social Services Departments attempt to invade the financial privacy of the individual. A form of this type may be considered a privacy rights violation in some states. An enlightened employer would turn this form over to the employee in question for proper disposition.

RE:

Gentlemen:

We are attempting to locate the above mentioned person in regards to a matter concerning the Department of Social Services. According to our information, this person was in your employ. Please examine your records and forward the following information:

Date Hired:__________ Still Employed:__________ Date Terminated:________

Social Security Number:____________ Gross Monthly Pay:________________

Last Known Address:____

Job Site:____

Number and Name of Dependents:________________ ________________

____

If subject has terminated, please forward name and address of new employer and of any inquiries made on this person.__________________

____

If you do not have a record of this person, please indicate and return this letter.

Your assistance is appreciated.

Sincerely,

Investigator

Office of Recovery Services
John P Abbott, Director

Salt Lake Office, 2250 South Redwood Road
Salt Lake City, Utah 84119
801-533-5068

The cautious sister steadfastly denied knowing her brother's location, but did offer to forward word in the event that he could be located.

The investigator cleverly set the trap, and the bait was dangling on the hook. For the first and only time, the sister then broke a "cardinal rule," and foolishly called her brother from her home phone. Several days later an official looking document generated by the Department of Recovery Services was sent to the telephone company. A copy of the sister's telephone bill was immediately forwarded to the investigator. A quick check of the long distance phone calls made from the sisters residence, and it was just a matter of time before this man who for years now had been living in the shadows, was reliving a near-forgotton nightmare.

Fortunately, his living in the shadows had bought him enough precious time so that the Statute of Limitations had just about run its course. He was thus saved from having to pay but a very small amount of his crippling financial obligations.

This is only one isolated example of the many extremes that Social Services investigators will avail themselves of in order to destroy the financial security of men residing in the shadows. The adversaries revel and gloat in their senseless, needless conquest of the financially depressed, divorced man on the run. They are not concerned that he may be burdened with an impossible financial task that a misinformed, uncaring legislative and judicial system has imposed on him. The fact that he is erroneously labeled a felon goes unheeded. His only crime is the lack of adequate finances to support two households.

Methods of Location

Unfortunately, our own Federal Government has joined the battle to subdue the persecuted male. In 1974, the United States Congress passed a little-known bill entitled "Public Law 93-647." The purpose of this legislation is to locate the persecuted male and provide this information to the various State Agencies. The end result of course is financial bondage for the disadvantaged male.

The bureaucratic justification behind this legislation is woman protectionism, and the high costs created by women on the welfare rolls. The law was fully implemented in 1977, with all fifty States participating.

The bill makes two provisions: first, it forces all States, under the threat of financial penalty, to establish Agencies to assist women collect past-due alimony and child support. The second provision is the enforcement and/or garnishment of salaries or pensions paid to US Civil Service or military personnel who are delinquent in child support or alimony. For additional information on this obviously male-oriented, highly discriminatory law write to:

The Office of Child Support
Department of Health, Education and Welfare
Washington, D.C. 20201.

If employed by the Federal Civil Service system or a member of the Armed Forces, write to:

The Office of Public Affairs
US Civil Service Commission
Washington D.C..

The investigator usually has access to a computer terminal, and can interrogate some of his own State's various data banks. Most of the other forty nine States, in addition to all Federal Agencies, are very sensitive and protective about the information they provide. However, most will cooperate fully with the Department of Recovery Services, and provide the history requested on any persecuted male. This is usually done in the form of a memo or letter to safeguard against wholesale invasion of computer memory devices.

The following is a complete listing of the methods used by the Social Services Investigators around the country in tracking down divorced males suspected of child support and/or alimony violations. The list is presented in descending order of usage and reliability.

Following the list is a detailing of each item that appears on the list.

Preferred methods used by the Social Services Investigator when tracking those wanted for past due child support or alimony are:

1. The informer - most often used and extremely dangerous
2. Proper, full, given name, (including nicknames)
3. Internal Revenue Service (Federal), an Agency gone wild
4. Social Security records, (Federal), nation-wide
5. Interest-bearing Financial Accounts watched by the IRS (a dead giveaway!).
6. Federal Payroll Tax reports, filed by the employer
7. Federal Income Tax reports, filed by the taxpayer
8. Military Service records, including the Veterans Administration.
9. Military Draft Registration, "Young Men, Uncle Sam wants you!"
10. Credit reports - apply for credit and lose your privacy
11. Credit Cards, Master Charge, and Visa, (Big Brother!)
12. Department of Motor Vehicles, drivers license and auto registration
13. Garbage - be careful of what gets thrown away
14. Children's school records - the innocent informers
15. Church membership - a congregation of innocent informers
16. Telephone Directory - listed AND unlisted numbers
17. State Payroll Tax reports - filed by the employer
18. State Income Tax reports - filed by the tax payer
19. US Post Office - mail forwarding address

20. US Passport
21. Bank records - cancelled checks
22. Stock certificates
23. Habit patterns - friends, hobbies, hangouts
24. Utilities applications
25. Employment records
26. Insurance records - including Government GI insurance
27. School records
28. Property tax rolls
29. Medical records - doctor and dentist
30. Federal and State licenses - Pilot, Meat Inspector, Barber, etc.
31. Unions and Fraternal Organizations, - organized labor can cause problems
32. Mailing lists
33. Voter registration

Interpretations

1. THE INFORMER is usually an ex-wife, neighbor, friend, or even a devoted relative. All of these are primary targets in order to help locate a missing male. Regardless of the painstaking efforts expended to successfully establish a new identity or disappearance, the informer should be considered to be the most dangerous and damaging of all! If trust is placed in any individual, human nature dictates the ever-present possibility of betrayal, even if done in a well-meaning and solicitous manner.

   It is easy to understand how much simpler the task of locating a persecuted male becomes with the assistance of an, albeit innocent, informer. The investigator's first step will always be to contact these possible informers.

2. PROPER FULL NAME is the next device the investigator will use in tracking a missing persecuted male. It is amazing how many are found simply by looking through a few phone books! The phone company maintains a nation-wide computerized filing system of every telephone subscriber in the country, whether the user is listed or unlisted! This information is made available to various State and Federal Agencies, and the Social Services investigator can therefore easily obtain this information.

3. INTERNAL REVENUE SERVICE, (IRS) can really be referred to as "Big Brother" when it comes to locating the persecuted male. Since practically all Americans are serialized via their Social Security number, the IRS presents a monumental threat because of the support it renders to all States in their search. Uncle Sam, in effect, is alienating millions of male tax payers, by joining with the States in this discriminatory action.

4. THE DEPARTMENT OF SOCIAL SECURITY, the IRS, and the Department of Health, Education and Welfare (HEW) are all bed partners when it comes to locating a "missing (male) parent." A common link between them is the bureaucracy known as the "Parent Locator Service," (PLS). By using the word "parent", this Federal Bureaucracy is attempting to disguise its actual discriminatory intent by insinuating that the PLS efforts are aimed at both sexes.

   The actual fact is, 99.99% of the PLS energies are targeted at the male species. The IRS, the Department of Social Security, and the records they keep, are all considered an open book to the Social Services investigator.

5. INTEREST-BEARING FINANCIAL ACCOUNTS, which includes checking, savings, stocks, bonds, etc., and any other interest-bearing financial service is closely monitored by the IRS for income someone might attempt to hide. These accounts are extremely dangerous because both names and Social Security numbers are supplied directly to the IRS. This information is made available to the investigator through the helping hand of the IRS.

   In addition to supplying parent locator information, the balance of these accounts might in jeopardy pending full investigation of the case.

6. FEDERAL PAYROLL TAX REPORTS, filed by the employer, are the reports that acutally enable the IRS to determine the tax payers whereabouts. These reports are submitted on a quarterly basis, or every three months. Each business in the United States is issued a Federal ID number. Each quarter, a report is submitted to the IRS. These reports identify the employee by name and Social Security number along with the amounts each employee has paid in Federal Taxes and Social Security insurance. This is the primary source of parent locator information and is freely passed on to the Department of Recovery Services.

7. FEDERAL INCOME TAX REPORTS, filled out by the taxpayer are used by the IRS as primary parent locater information, and must verify the reports as filed by the employer. Both reports must coincide.

8. MILITARY RECORDS, information from all branches of the Armed Forces are made available to the Parent Locator Service. Those persecuted males serving Uncle Sam in any branch of the military can easily be financially cornered by an ex-wife and tormented until discharged. Any individual serving our country under these depressing conditions is unlikely to find relief until his military career ends. Career advancements may be witheld, as well as a devastating portion of any salary or bonus.

9. FEDERAL DRAFT REGISTRATION places those unfortunate young men who must, by law, register for the draft "between a rock and a hard spot." The United States Government has been coerced by womens' protectionists into providing draft registration information to the Parent Locator Service. This, in fact, should be considered to be an unconscionable and traitorous act against the patriotic young men who are volunteering to serve their country!

10. CREDIT RATING REPORTS, includes files numbered in excess of 150 million in computer storage devices. Of the over two thousand credit bureaus in the country, five have virtually monopolized this service. Credit Bureau, Inc., (CBI) is a division of Equifax, Inc. This conglomerate has approximately one hundred million personal files, TRW Credit Data about seventy five million individual files. Chilton Corporation, Trans Union Systems, and Associated Credit Services have combined files equal to, or larger than, Equifax. These credit rating companies also share computer data among one another. What it actually means is a huge, nationwide data base containing vital information on an overwhelming majority of American citizens. This information is not adequately protected and can be accessed by almost anyone.

11. CREDIT CARDS go hand in hand with credit rating (above). These small, innocent pieces of plastic can and do leave a trail that can lead directly to a persecuted male who uses them. These cards provide hard copy information which has been used in countless instances as court evidence by an exwife's attorney. Spending habits and life style thus become an open book to the investigator.

12. DEPARTMENT OF MOTOR VEHICLES, drivers license data, State ID cards, and auto registration information are all good secondary sources for tracking down persecuted males. The major problem facing the investigator is that the information is only State-wide. Some States cooperate in the search, but the process is often slow and unreliable.

    Responses are usually handled by mail since these Departments are not capable or willing to share computer data. This information is not confidential and can be obtained by anyone making a request.

13. GARBAGE. Very few people consider the serious implications of what information is contained in their garbage! From trash, a whole life style can inadvertently be revealed. Old letters, cancelled checks, bank receipts, phone bills, credit card statements, etc. can all incriminate, the list is endless! A good investigator always avails himself of a suspect's garbage on garbage pick-up day! Picking up garbage is not a violation of the law and is there for the

taking. Those desiring personal privacy usually burn sensitive material. Some transport their entire load of garbage to an alternate site such as a commercial dumpster.

14. CHILDREN'S SCHOOL RECORDS are considered by the investigator to be an excellent source of information, as are the children themselves. The Department of Recovery Services will not stop at violating a family's privacy in gathering the information they desire.

    They usually use a school authority such as a teacher or even a principal question the targeted student for information concerning their father. In a divorced family (or broken home), this is often a very sensitive subject for a young child and can result in a degrading, demeaning, and traumatic experience for the young students. The older students usually feels they are betraying a loved family member (in this case the father), by answering these questions.

15. CHURCH MEMBERSHIP, or religious affiliations, are sometimes used by the more energetic investigator, but only after the previous methods have proved fruitless.

16. THE TELEPHONE DIRECTORY is considered an excellent primary source of tracing information if used in conjuction with the listings maintained by the telephone company. It is discussed in more detail under "Proper Full Name".

17. STATE PAYROLL TAX REPORTS as filed by an employer are limited by State boundaries, and are not considered a primary, or even reliable, source, for location, if the persecuted male has left the State. However, since both the Federal (IRS), and State Income Tax Departments cooperate with one another, caution is required.

18. STATE INCOME TAX REPORTS, filed by the taxpayer, are also confined to State borders and are used only as a secondary source of information. Since some States share tax information, caution is required.

19. US Post Office. Mail forwarding address records are kept only by the Post Office branch where the information was filed. For any persecuted male to leave a correct forwarding address can therefore result in a fatal error!

20. US Passport. It is unknown at this time if any cooperation exists between the General Passport Office and the Parent Locator Service. Since little information is available it would be best to assume there is support between the two.

21. Bank Records and cancelled checks are considered "fair game" by the IRS. A court order or even the account holder's prior notification is not required for the Federal

Government to examine this information. Cancelled checks leave an undesirable paper trail to assets and lifestyle, and are an open door for invasion of personal privacy.

22. Stock Certificates and transactions pertaining to them may involve earnings or income that is constantly monitored by the IRS.

23. through 33. These sources of tracking information normally fall under the catagory of miscellaneous methods, and even though they might prove usefull to the investigator, they will normally be used only as a last resort.

The Statute of Limitations

The one bright prospect that glimmers off in the distance to aid many a persecuted male is the "Statute of Limitations" law of the fifty States. The Statute of Limitations is a State or Federal law restricting the time within which a legal action can be commenced.

In other words, an ex-wife has only a prescribed amount of time during which she can collect for past due child support or alimony amounts. If unsuccessful for too long a period, the financial obligation may be dismissed.

All States have a Statute of Limitations law for past due child support and alimony payments. The Statute of Limitations laws vary widely between States, and are constantly being changed by State legislators. These laws are of prime importance to the persecuted male. It is advisable that any man with a substantial amount of past due child support or alimony consult with an attorney concerning these laws.

Unfortunately, any Statute of Limitations law can be tolled (suspended) by certain acts. This means that although the time limit within which one can bring an action is counted from a certain date, its running can, and often is postponed until the occurrence of some event which is specified by law. Again, check with a good attorney for whatever possible tolls might be in effect.

Some Good Advice

Most men love their children dearly and have a sincere desire to remain an integral part of their lives and provide for them. In turn, these same fathers have a right to supply themselves with the basic essentials of life. If it becomes impossible to accomplish both, a man in the shadows may be compelled to make some financial modifications in order to survive. It is strongly advised that the father not become overly stressed and discontinue financial assistance altogether. Provide what can realistically be afforded.

This may be considerably less than the court-ordered amount, but an honest effort is generally considered in a positive fashion by most courts.

There is no sympathy offered to the father who maintains a high life style for himself while refusing to help with the financial needs of his children. Decisions must be made on financial capabilities, not court-ordered impossibilities!

The persecuted male should not feel alone and helpless if subjected to excessive child support or abusive alimony payments. Millions of men are in the same circumstances.

The option for freedom from financial bondage is a difficult decision to make and must be made carefully since financial freedom and personal survival usually are at stake.

CHAPTER 3

PRE-FADE TECHNIQUES

1. About Those Undercover
2. The Overview
3. Calm Down, Cool Off
4. How to Select a Winning Lawyer
5. Dealing with the Process Server
6. Establishing a Contact
7. Setting up the Mail Drop
8. Moving and Storing Personal Belongings
9. Choosing a New Location
10. The Right Living Quarters
11. Applying for a New Job
12. Forged and Counterfeit Documents
13. Self-Generated Documents
14. A Word about Computers

About Those Undercover

Chapters 3 through 7 are the results of an independant study conducted in Southern California during 1981 and 1982, using 153 divorced men, and interviewing them in depth. They originated from all sections of the country. About two-thirds of them were fathers with one or more children, the remaining were from childless marriages. Their ages ranged from 20 to 56, their salaries from between $14,000 to $42,000. Most of the men in the upper salary brackets came from childless marriages and refused to pay any alimony. Some were quite hostile toward their ex-wife and the Government in general. Of those interviewed, most were living under assumed names with either forged, counterfeit, or borrowed documents. Virtually all of them were trying to escape the financial burden of excessive child support or alimony.

As the interviews progressed it became obvious that the art of living underground had become a precise science with many of them, with 103 considering their actions necessary for their financial survival.

Of the 102 men with children, 87 claimed their actions would not be necessary if automatic joint, physical custody of minor children was the law of the land. The same majority condoned supporting their children on their own without dividing their income between two households. 47 continued to pay reduced amounts of child support, the remainder paid none.

23 of those men coming from childless marriages were paying reduced amounts of alimony, the remainder refused to pay any.

The term "living in a fade" was coined during the interviews. The three methods of fading, as well as the pre-fade techniques outlined in this book (with some variations) are those developed by the participants in the study.

The following chapters represent the results of those interviews, and the actual methods used by the men to gain financial freedom.

The Overview

The ultimate goal of many persecuted males is the restoration of personal dignity coupled with financial privacy. This is accomplished by leaving any pursuers confused as to his whereabouts. Unless a massive turnabout takes place in the present Civil Divorce laws, the option of "fading" may be a persecuted man's only option for financial survival.

The previous chapter listed the numerous methods available to the Social Services investigators to locate those attempting to escape the financial bondage of excessive child support or alimony. The following chapters are devoted to show how many of these methods are neutralized to effectively enhance their personal privacy.

The successful fade is totally dependent on how carefully a man plans and executes the begining stages! The least successful are those who allow themselves to panic, and who flee from the unjust financial burdens without having made the proper, and often lengthy preparations necessary for a successful fade. They usually move to a new location, change jobs, and after doing this feel that their financial security is assured because of the new surroundings.

Any persecuted male who plans a future life on this type of shaky foundation is foolhardy and failure is virtually assured!

Some men assume that the greater the distance, the greater the security. Nothing could be further from the truth!

Also, there are the self-proclaimed experts who go so far as to change their name, legally or illegally, and who then are astonished at how rapidly they are nontheless discovered.

There are basically three separate and distinct methods of fading; each has its own inherent advantages. Each method has a particular goal to accomplish. The three categories of fading are classified as the "temporary fade," "partial fade," and the "complete fade." Each of the three methods of fading will be discussed in detail in later chapters.

Calm Down, Cool Off

Panic is your most dangerous enemy! Even when under extreme financial pressures to pay excessive alimony or child support, the one thing to always remember is: **DO NOT PANIC!** The reasoning here is obvious. A persecuted male, being human, when threatened with legal action will often rush headlong into a faulty plan without ample forethought. Such hasty actions invariably result in failure and make the job of the investigator far too simple. Legal procedures as a rule are quite slow! Take advantage of this precious time to correctly prepare for a successful departure. The temporary fade is ideally suited for men in a hurry. It is extremely simple to effect and was designed to be accomplished quickly. It may involve a change of scenery and a new job, but for many it's the only means available for survival at the moment.

How To Select A Winning Lawyer

The present day credibility of those engaged in the law profession is at an all-time low. Attorney's today have a reputation envied by no one. There is no single group of professionals as disdained as lawyers! However, it is not the intent of this book to either add to, or detract from, that reputation.

One of the most important tasks any male involved in family litigation may want to resolve is how and where to acquire the services of a reliable, qualified, caring attorney. Beware of the "Lawyer Referral Services" located in the yellow pages of the telephone directory. That service is generated and supported by the lawyers themselves. These advertisments cannot be relied upon because they are generally the results of new attorneys attempting to drum up business.

The State Bar Association will suggest names of those who specialize in family law, but this too is considered a poor method of selecting an attorney. The State Bar Association will not recommend just the top performers, because that would show preference, and the State Bar Association will not engage in this practice.

There are several danger signals that indicate a loser and they must be strictly adhered to when shopping for an attorney.

Beware of the attorney whose initial consultation is very brief, and who then quickly refers his potential client to another member of the firm. If both attorneys are specializing in the same segment of the law, the client usually is being "pushed off" to a junior member of the firm who has little or no experience, and has therefore not yet established a good track record. He therefore cannot be relied upon to handle the case effectivly! Don't waste valuable time and money on this type of lawyer!

Some negative indications to look out for: the attorney who acts hurried, busy, and cuts the initial consultation short saying he'll be at the court house a few minutes prior to the actual court date to review the details.

Any attorney who is unwilling to take what time is needed and ask the necessary questions is unable to prepare himself for a first-rate case, and should be avoided at all costs. This type is only interested in his fee; he wants to expend no more energy on a case than absolutely necessary. A definite loser!

As a general rule, do not engage an attorney who enjoys a high success ratio representing women in divorce actions. Like it or not, his type has already demonstrated his allegiance to the female sex and would have some degree of difficulty to emotionally accept the plight of the male. The case would surely suffer from a lack of enthusiasm.

The most accurate and reliable method of locating an attorney to fit one's needs is through reputation and track record. Ask those who are involved in regular court activities such as court clerks, court recorders, police officers, or even a friend who is seasoned in court activities, whom they recommend. The lawyer selected is vitally important to one's cause, no one can afford to engage a losing attorney!

Additional assistance in the selection of a qualified attorney may be obtained from one of the organized Fathers Groups now springing up all over the country. These groups can be invaluable in helping the divorced male solve many of his legal and emotional problems.

Dealing With The Process Server

Service is defined in legal practice as the act of showing or delivering a legal document such as an Injunction, a Notice, a Summons, or a Writ to a person, thereby officially notifying him of a legal proceeding that involves him. Service of process, as it is called, must be made by a legally authorized person.

As with most other laws, those concerning process service vary greatly among the fifty states, but the goals are similar. If properly served, the recipient is officially notified that he must appear at a prescribed time and place, usually under the jurisdiction of a particular court system. If one decides to ignore the summons and refuses to appear, a warrent for arrest may be issued.

Any man who finds himself behind in child support or alimony payments should be on guard against the sudden and unwanted intrusion of the "Process Server. " When dealing with one, if you are not served with papers, there is no requirement to appear. If improperly served, a good attorney can have the summons quashed.

The process server is usually paid a pitiful wage for his services. He usually receives all, or a portion of, the service fee paid by the plaintiff. Some service fees are as low as $10.00; making him earn his money is a procedure practiced by many.

Generally the process server is required to use his own personal automobile and provide his own expenses in tracking down a defendant. Any profit comes only after he has succeeded in his obligation to locate and serve the recepient. Allowing him to literally wear himself out in as many unsuccessful service attempts as possible is a strategy frequently used by his intended victims. If enough attempts to complete service result in failure, it not only aids in demoralizing the server, but may discourage additional and future efforts as well. It also places a financial burden on behalf of the the plaintiff, not to mention the added inconvenience of court date postponements arranged by your ex-wife's attorney.

The individuals employed as process servers do not hold a position of much envy; many of them are frustrated would-be law enforcement officers. Some States permit the strengthening of a process server's image and restore bent egos by supplying some sort of official looking ID card along with a companion badge. Some are issued a uniform of sorts. Fringe benefits of this type often attract the emotionally disturbed individual who feeds on a desparate need to display and wield authority.

Process servers are generally considered an "unsavory lot" with little regard for the personal privacy of others, and often resort to bending the law for their own benefit. Some even attempt to intimidate a "Servee" (defendant) into accepting a summons by flashing a badge as if he/she were a law enforcement officer. As a general rule they are not employed by the state. They are usually provided by private enterprise, or county and/or local branches of Government. The qualifications for a process server are usually specified by the State Legislature. Some states simply require that an individual be at least 18 years of age as the only requirement or qualification!

Many States also use the services of local police officers or constables to deliver a summons. These officers are generally off duty and are "moonlighting" to earn extra cash. Even though a process server may be plying his trade in official uniform, avoidance seems to be the watch-word.

Be aware of the impending dangers of facing a process server. In an attempt to complete service, a server's first concern will always be to verify the identity of the individual whom he is serving. For example, he may ask: "is your name John Smith?" If one should answer in the affirmative, he will then quickly be handed the summons. If the intended recipient refuses to accept the document, the server then places it at his feet or on the door step.

He can then signify under oath or by written statement that the prospective defendant has been duly notified of impending legal action against him.

Seasoned veterans are prepared for these suprise encounters by immediately denying any knowledge of the person in question. If surprised at home, they might respond with: "who are you looking for?", and "You must be at the wrong address," for this alone can work wonders! A doormat inscribed with a name other than the correct one placed at the front door has also been successful. Another method often used is that of placing a fictitous name on the mail box. Since the post office delivers to an address and not a name, mail will still be delivered correctly.

Mailbox contents are often examined by unscrupulous process servers and one's mailbox should therefore be kept locked, in order to keep prying eyes away from incriminating information. The mail drop system is usually used to provide the needed privacy.

Some servers will call on the telephone (if the number is available) prior to an actual visit. Telephone answering machines can be used to effectively disguise true identity if desired.

Many men anticipate the possibility of these events and prepare in advance a very convincing cover story in addition to self-generated ID for verification. A process server cannot legally demand ID, he may attempt to bluff one into voluntarily showing some ID, but he is on dangerous, not legal, ground.

One persecuted male who denied being the owner of his legal name was ordered to provide ID by an unusually obnoxious and determined server who had repeatedly rung his front door bell. The intended recipient informed him he was in violation of constitutional law in demanding ID from a private citizen. He then demanded the name and ID of the server, and indicated an official complaint would be filed. Realizing his bluff had failed, the server retreated, never to be seen or heard from again.

A large portion of a lawyer's income is very dependent on just how successful the server is in serving an intended receipient. Since most civil court cases require that both a plaintiff and a defendant be present in order to commence with legal proceedings, the value of the server becomes obvious. Unfortunately, lawyers conveniently forget to advise clients on their legal rights as far as a process server is concerned. They usually steer clear of giving even a hint of how a process server can be thwarted.

Some States permit the process server to place the summons in the hands of secondary persons, someone other than the intended recipient. This may include a family member or a co-worker. The dangers here are obvious! The secondary person may forget, or never bother to inform the intended recipient of the summons. Under these conditions, an uninformed defendant might get arrested for ignoring a summons he knows nothing about!

When a persecuted male suspects that unwanted litigation is headed his way, he must inform his secondary persons that they have not been authorized to accept legal documents on his behalf. Most are told to verbalize these facts to anyone attempting to deliver such documents. This is the same method used by attorneys in protecting a client against unwanted service.

All of these methods of serving a summons fall under the category of "Personal Service." That is, the process server delivers the documents in person to the person sought by law.

The most innocent, and by far the most used means of serving a summons is called the "substituted," or "constructive" methods. Under these methods, the summons is delivered by "certified," or "registered" mail. Any persecuted male suspecting possible legal action against him never accepts mail that requires a signature! The mail is refused simply by telling the postman that one will not accept delivery, which is perfectly legal. Without a signature, the mail will be returned to the originator. When refusing this type of mail it is vitally important that the intended recipient obtain the name and address of the sender. This is valuable information and will reveal exactly who the pursuer is and where he is coming from. The postman or delivery person will normally gladly provide this information.

Some attorneys are brazen enough to send a summons through regular mail, but most recipients are wise enough to send such mail back to the sender unopened, perhaps even using rubber stamps to enhance the act with messages such as "addressee not at this address, return to sender," or "deceased," etc. If a summons is sent by common mail, the sending attorney has no verification that such mail was actually delivered and/or received, and he would therefore have difficulty proving proper "service".

Do not fall victim to the mistaken belief that a summons is always issued by a court and signed by a judge! Attorneys usually generate summons on their own, thus compelling one to appear as stated. An ex-wife's attorney will probably be responsible for the generation of a summons, if one is behind in child support or alimony.

Some attorneys resort to very clever methods of serving a summons on an unsuspecting male. One of the most devious methods reported is that of the attorney who sends out summons to the "difficult male" via United Parcel Service (UPS) in a large box. Of course, delivery of the package requires a signature!

An informed persecuted male can stay ahead of litigations headed in his direction without actually being served, and without arousing the awareness of those trying to serve him. This is accomplished by obtaining the original case number from the divorce file. This number may be discovered on the divorce decree, or any other court papers involved in the original case. Helpful information can also be gained from attempted deliveries of suspected registered or certified mail, namely, the return address and name of sender.

Armed with this information, a copy of the summons can be obtained from the County Recorder's Office (either in the ex-wife's residential County, or the County where the divorce originated). These files are open for public inspection and clerks are on duty to assist in locating the information needed. If the correct file cannot be located, the clerks will assist with other means of finding the proper file. Many persecuted men, as a means of self protection, find it wise not to correctly identify themselves to the records clerks. In this manner the intended recipient can get a hard copy of the actual summons without being officially served.

Two proccesses should never be observed by those who suffer from a weak stomach, the first being the "making of sausage," and the second, "laws being passed," as exhibited in the next paragraph.

These are the two most disturbing methods of serving legal notices. They consist of "notification by publication," (or just sending a letter to the Court Clerk). These particular methods demonstrate exactly how pagan some of our laws are. Notification by publication is accomplished by placing a notice in practically any newspaper (usually the smaller and more obscure the publication, the better!), and then continuing on with litigation against the defendant without his presence or knowledge. This is a typical example of laws passed by lawyers serving as legislators to benefit themselves and make their jobs easier!

Since the defendant had no opportunity to defend himself in court, a good attorney can often get a new trial.

Notification by publication is the method generally used by an ex-wife's attorney to start an adoption (stealing) process of an absentee father's children. Many fathers, forced from their homes and separated from their children, are further humiliated and degraded by the adoption of his children, usually by the ex-wife's new husband. A small ad in some remote, little-read newspaper proclaims to its readers that the absentee father has been removed from the position of being the legal father and guardian, and will be replaced by a State appointed guardian. No Government Agency, be it State, or Federal, has the moral right to dispossess a father of his natural children. It is disgusting and repugnant laws such as these which will eventually destroy voluntary compliance with the present judicial system.

In the "letter to the court clerk" method, a letter is filed by the plaintiff's (ex-wife's) attorney, indicating that all other methods to serve the defendant have failed. As with the "notification by publication" method, the court proceedings go on without the presence of the male in question. Since there was no opportunity for defense, a new trial is always a possibility.

Establishing A Contact

A word of caution. The section on the Informer should be foremost in one's mind when to selecting a contact. A contact is not absolutely essential to a successful fade, but it can be a valuable enhancement when the need arises.

A "Contact," by definition, is an individual designated to "aid and assist" the man in the shadows. The main function of a contact is to serve as an observer and information source. If the man residing in the shadows has children, he will no doubt want to maintain contact with them. This is usually accomplished through the use of a dedicated contact. A contact also keeps the father abreast of any legal manuverings against him. A contact will keep him posted on important events such as births, weddings, social events, and deaths, etc,. Also, valuable legal documents may be handled and processed by a capable contact.

As should be obvious, a contact must be a loyal friend who is in complete sympathy with, and allied to, one's cause. When selecting a contact, one must rely on one's best judgement. Extreme caution must prevail, or the plan to launch a successful fade could collapse like a "House of Cards." Usually, a close relative is chosen as the best prospect to serve as a contact. A sister or mother might be the best choice.

A single person generally makes a better contact than a married one. The reason is obvious. Married couples are likely to share secrets, and this enhances the chance of exposing the whole plan.

It is best if the contact reacts well under pressure. If a contact is engaged for an extended length of time, he or she is likely to become exposed to some "heat" from one or more bureaucratic agencies in the area. If the contact is informed and knows what to expect, he/she might anticipate such encounters as an adventuresome challenge, rather than a frightening happening.

Most males living in a fade reward their contact. They make it a habit to leave a sufficient deposit to cover out-of-pocket expenses that may occur, such as postage, copying charges, reimbursements for automobile expenses, etc. A reward in the way of small personal gifts also is well worthwhile. Money may be offered, but it may be rejected if the person serving as the contact is sufficiently allied to the cause.

A contact is instructed never to accept or sign for any legal documents without prior permission. This includes certified or registered mail arriving in the sought person's name. Should a suspected process server attempt to serve unwanted documents, such papers should be refused. The contact is instructed to advise the server that he/she is not authorized to accept or forward such documents. The contact should then make an effort to obtain the case number and the originator. The server may not cooperate with this request, but it's worth a try. As described in the section "Dealing with the Process Server," the case number is extremely valuable data.

The contact is instructed to <u>never</u>, ever, phone the man in the shadows from his or her home telephone! If a phone call becomes necessary, a pay phone must be used. Telephone credit cards also <u>are</u> <u>not</u> used for these calls, ever!

Regardless of how dependable a contact is, males living in a fade must <u>never</u> reveal data on their post-fade employers. It is not even essential that the contact be informed of his new residential address. Under adverse conditions, a contact, if exposed, can be summoned into court and forced to testify on information concerning the individual being protected. Therefore, most males living in a fade tell their contact as little as possible. The mail drop system should be relied on for primary communications between the two parties.

The contact must also be cautioned about the indiscriminate disposal of garbage, because of the revealing information it may contain. The same precautions should be observed that are covered in the section "Methods of Location" found elsewhere in this book.

Setting Up The Mail Drop

The mail drop is another term for private mailhandling services. There are three basic types of mail service. The first type is the "mail pick-up" service. This is simply a secondary address where mail can be picked up in person or by an appointed designee. The second is "mail forwarding." Mail is received, repackaged, and forwarded to the proper person. The third type uses the "double envelope procedure", whereby the mail service re-mails all mail gathered into one big envelope to be forwarded to the intended recipient. Good mail services usually provide all three types of service, the object being that mail processing is relativly safe from the watchful eyes of the unintended.

The primary purpose of a mail drop is to cover and disguise one's actual location in addition to creating deceptions if so desired. If a man in the shadows intends to appear as if he was living in

INSTRUCTIONS

INSTRUCTIONS: Complete Items 1 through 9 and the address on front of form. Please print, except for Item 8 which **requires your** signature.

1. Check only one block. If the entire family is moving from the old address, check entire family block. If a member of the family remains at the old address with the same last name, check individual move block and fill out a separate change of address order form for each person moving from the old household. If the move is for a business, check the block marked business.

2. Indicate the date which you want mail forwarding to begin.

3. If your move is **TEMPORARY** (you will be returning to your original household within twelve months) indicate the date to discontinue mail forwarding. If you fail to fill out this date, your mail will be treated as a permanent order and will continue to be forwarded.

4. Print **ONLY ONE** last name of person(s) moving to the same address. If person(s) with the same last name are moving from the same old address to different new addresses, use separate forms. If this is a business move, print name of business. If more than one business is moving, separate forms must be completed.

5. If you have checked individual in Item 1, print first name of individual moving. If you have checked family move, print first name of the head of household, and include middle name or initials if they are commonly used. If business move, leave this item blank.

6. Print complete **OLD** address. If your **OLD** address is a rural route (RR), include the box number in the designated space. The abbreviation RR/HCR No. stands for Rural Route/ Highway Contract Route Number. If your **OLD** address includes an apartment number, please provide it.

7. Print complete **NEW** address. If your **NEW** address is a Rural Route, include the box number in the proper space. If your **NEW** address includes an apartment number, it is needed for accurate mail delivery.

8. This change of address order is not valid without your signature. See note on front of form.

9. Self-explanatory.
COMPLETE ADDRESS PORTION ON FRONT OF FORM

Sample change of address card
required by the US Post office
for mail forwarding.

U.S. Postal Service
CHANGE OF ADDRESS ORDER

Customer Instructions: Complete Items 1 thru 9. Except Item 8, please PRINT all information including address on face of card.

OFFICIAL USE ONLY

Zone/Route ID No.

Date Entered on Form 3982
M M D D Y Y

Expiration Date
M M D D Y Y

Clerk/Carrier Endorsement

1. Change of Address for *(Check one)* ☐ Individual ☐ Entire Family ☐ Business

2. Start Date — Month Day Year

3. If TEMPORARY address, print date to discontinue forwarding — Month Day Year

4. Print Last Name or Name of Business *(If more than one, use separate Change of Address Order Form for each)*

5. Print First Name of Head of Household *(include Jr., Sr., etc.)*. Leave blank if the Change of Address Order is for a business.

6. Print **OLD** mailing address, number and street *(if Puerto Rico, include urbanization zone)*

Apt./Suite No. P.O. Box No. R.R/HCR No. Rural Box/HCR Box No.

City State ZIP Code

7. Print **NEW** mailing address, number and street *(if Puerto Rico, include urbanization zone)*

Apt./Suite No. P.O. Box No. R.R/HCR No. Rural Box/HCR Box No.

City State ZIP Code

8. Signature *(See conditions on reverse)*

9. Date Signed — Month Day Year

OFFICIAL USE ONLY

OFFICIAL USE ONLY

Verification Endorsement

PS Form 3575, Mar 1988

★USGPO-1988-210-546

INSTRUCTIONS FOR WORKING COMBINATION BOX

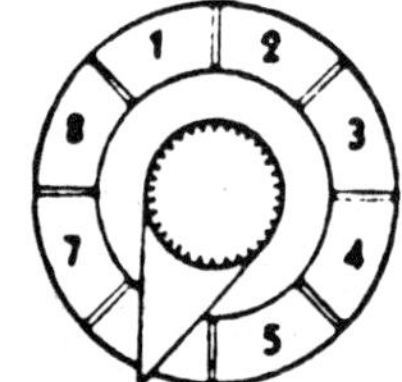

1. Clear dial by three revolutions to the right, stop on ________
2. Turn dial to the left and stop the second time around on ______
3. Turn right and stop at ________________
4. Turn latch key LEFT to open.

Your ZIP + 4 is:

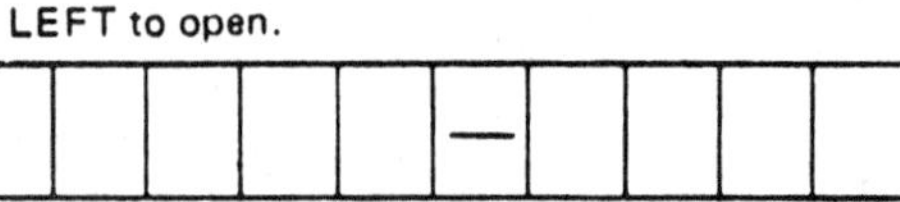

Rules for use of Post Office Box and Caller Service

IMPORTANT: Post Office Box and Caller Service are Subject to the following and the regulations in Parts 951 and 952 *DMM.*

I. Mail, which is properly addressed to a post office box or caller service number, will be delivered through that post office box or caller service for

Individual boxholders or callers, or anyone residing in their household.

A firm, corporation, association, or public or private, institution, or any one associated with the organization. . . . . .

II. Customers should promptly notify correspondents of their current box or caller number address.

III. Post Office Box or caller service fees are to be paid in advance for one or two semiannual periods. A notice of fees due will be placed in a box or included with caller mail 20 days before the due date. If a boxholder is out of town and has submitted a temporary forwarding order, the notice will be mailed to the temporary address. It is the responsibility of the boxholder to assure that payment is made on time. If payment is sent by mail, it must be received by the postmaster by the due date. Payment may be by cash or by check payable to the postmaster. Do not send cash by mail. If a check is returned by the bank, the box will be closed until that check is made good.

IV. If fee is not paid on time, the post office box will be secured so that mail cannot be removed through the door. If box rent or caller fees are not paid after 10 days, mail will be removed and treated as undeliverable, unless forwarded on a change of address order. Closed post office boxes will be immediately available to new customers.

V. Post office boxes or caller service may not be used for any purpose prohibited by Postal Regulations. (See Parts 951 and 952 *Domestic Mail Manual. (DMM).*

VI. Boxes and caller numbers may not be used for the sole purpose of having the Postal Service forward or transfer mail to another address free of charge.

VII. Boxholders shall promptly remove mail, or have it removed, from their boxes. Advance arrangements must be specifically made with the postmaster if mail is to be accumulated for more than 30 days and an overflow condition is probable.

VIII. Keys for key-type post office boxes will be issued upon payment of $1 for each key, including those initially issued for each post office box. When a box is surrendered, the Postal Service will repurchase a maximum of two keys. Keys for post office box may be obtained only from the Postal Service.

IX. Customers who use post office box or caller service, are required to maintain a current Form 1093. *Application for Post Office Box or Caller Service,* on file with the Postal Service. Any information on the application, which changes or becomes obsolete, must be corrected by promptly updating the Form 1093 on file with the postmaster at the office where the post office box or caller service is used.

X. A box may be closed or caller service terminated as provided in Parts 951 and 952 *DMM.*

The customer may appeal a closure in writing to higher authority by following the detailed procedures in Sections 951.84 and 952.44 *DMM.*

XI. Concerning information required for the completion of this form:

A. The collection of this information is authorized by 39 U.S.C. 403,404.

B. This information will be used to provide the applicant with post office box or caller service.

C. This information may be routinely disclosed:

1. To persons authorized by law to serve judicial process for the purpose of serving such process.
2. To a government agency, when necessary for the performance of its duties.
3. To anyone, when the box is being used for the purpose of doing or soliciting business with the public.
4. To a Congressional Office, at the request of the boxholder.
5. In response to a subpoena or court order.
6. Where pertinent to a legal proceeding in which the Postal Service is a party.

D. Completion of this form is voluntary; however, if this information is not provided, the applicant will be unable to use a box or receive caller service.

XII. Customers are referred to Parts 951 and 952 *DMM* for a more detailed explanation of these regulations.

PS Form **1093**, Dec. 1986 **(PART III)**

☆ USGPO 1987- 172-181/59310

Sample application for a regular P.O. box at the US Post Office.

CUSTOMER: Complete Items 1, 3-7, 15 and 19 (Item 2 for P.O. Use ONLY)

1. Name to which box number(s) is(are) assigned	2. Box/Caller Nos. ________ Thru ________
3. Name of person making application *(If representing an organization, show title and name)*	
4. Will this box be used for soliciting or doing business with the public? *(Check one)* a. ☐ YES b. ☐ NO	
5. Address *(No., Street, City, State and ZIP Code. Record address change on reverse and line out address below.)*	6. Telephone No. *(If any)*

APPLICANT PLEASE NOTE: Execution of this application signifies your agreement to comply with all postal rules relative to Post Office boxes or caller service.

7. Signature of applicant *(Same as Item 3)*	8. Date of application

ITEMS 8-15: TO BE COMPLETED BY POST OFFICE

9. Type of identification *(Driver's license military identification, other; show identification no.)*	10. Eligibility for carrier-delivery ☐ CITY ☐ RURAL ☐ NONE	11. Box size needed

12. Dates of Service		13. Service Assigned	14. Information Verified by
a. Started	b. Ended	a. ☐ Post Office Box b. ☐ Caller c. ☐ Reserve Number	a. *(Initials)*

Use separate card for each number or inclusive group of numbers, and type of service. File Part I alphabetically by Customer's Name.

PS Form 1093, Dec. 1986 **(PART I) APPLICATION FOR POST OFFICE BOX OR CALLER SERVICE**

CUSTOMER: Complete Items 15 and 19.

SPECIAL ORDERS	ITEMS 16-18: TO BE COMPLETED BY POST OFFICE
15. Postmaster: The following named persons, or authorized representatives of the organizations listed are authorized to accept mail addressed to this(these) post office box or caller number(s). Continue on reverse if necessary. ☐ Check if reverse is used.	16. Post Office Box/Caller number for which this card is applicable ________ through ________
	17. ☐ Check if box is to be used for Express Mail reshipment.
a. Applicant *(Same as Item 3)*	18. Post Office ... Date Stamp
b. Name in which box rented *(Same as Item 1)*	
c. Other	
d. Other	
CUSTOMER NOTE: Possession of post office box Key or combination may be considered by the Postal Service to be valid evidence that possessor is authorized to remove mail from boxes.	19. I have read instructions and will comply Signature of Applicant *(Same as Item 3)*

Use separate card for each number or inclusive group of numbers, and type of service. File Part II by box or caller number.

PS Form 1093, Dec. 1986 **(PART II) APPLICATION FOR POST OFFICE BOX OR CALLER SERVICE**

U.S. POSTAL SERVICE

APPLICATION FOR DELIVERY OF MAIL THROUGH AGENT

1. Date

In consideration of delivery of my or our mail to the agent named below, the addressee and agent agree that: (1) the Postal Service will not forward my or our mail on a change of address order upon termination of this agency relationship; (2) the forwarding or return of my or our mail is the responsibility of the agent; and (3) all mail, including letters and other first class mail, delivered to the agent under this authorization must be prepaid with new postage when redeposited in the mails.

NOTE: This publication must be executed in duplicate by applicant in the presence of the agent, his authorized employee or a notary public. A signed copy will be kept on file by the agent in such manner that it is at all times available for examination by postal representatives.

TO: **Postmaster**

APPLICANT IDENTIFICATION

D/L ____________

C/Card ____________

Other ____________

Bus. Phone ____________

Res. Phone ____________

PRIVACY ACT: The collection of this information is authorized by 39 USC' 403, 404. It serves as the written authority for the delivery of mail other than as addressed. As a routine use, this information may be disclosed to an appropriate law enforcement agency for investigative or prosecution proceedings, to a congressional office at your request, to a labor organization as required by the NLRA, and where pertinent, in a legal proceeding to which the Postal Service is a party. Completion of this form is voluntary, however, if this information is not provided the mail will be withheld from delivery to the agent and delivered to the addressee, or, if the address of the addressee is that of the agent, returned to the sender.

2. Mail addressed to (*Name, address and ZIP Code*)

3. Deliver to and in care of (*Name, address and ZIP code of agent*)

4. Name of applicant (*Print or type*)

4a. Home address (*Number, street and ZIP code*)

5. Name of firm or corporation

5a. Business address (*Name, street and ZIP code*)

6. Kind of business

7. *If address is a FIRM, name each member whose mail is to be delivered*

8. *If a CORPORATION, give names and addresses of its officers*

Sample application for a P.O. box from a private vendor.

9. Reference (*Name, address and ZIP code*)

10. Reference (*Name, address and ZIP code*)

11. If business name of the address (*Corporation or Trade Name*) has been registered, give name of county and state, and date of registration.

12. Signature of agent

13. Signature of applicant (*If firm or corporation, application must be signed by officer. Show title.*)

PS Form 1583, Nov. 1982

☆ USGPO 1987 - 181-700/55537

Omaha, Nebraska, when he is actually residing in Southern California, use of a mail service makes this possible. Just send a double envelope letter from Southern California, to a mail drop in Omaha. The mail service, upon receiving the double letter, will remove the inner envelope and re-mail it. The recipient then gets a letter, or package that has the postmark of Omaha, Nebraska. This feature has proven extremely valuable in creating a smoke screen and confusing trackers, especially the IRS. Federal tax returns are often sent to distant IRS processing centers from strategically located mail drops as an aid to preserve privacy. A place of residence is effectively concealed by substituting the mail drop address in place of the actual one.

There are hundreds of reliable mail forwarding services located throughout the fifty states and Canada as well as overseas. A mail drop, if properly handled, is not only reasonably secure, but an absolute must for corresponding with a contact. The mail drop is also used for receiving important documents such as birth certificates, drivers licenses, ID cards, tax returns, etc.

The first step in setting up a mail drop is a search through the yellow pages directory of the city where the mail drop is to be located. Under the heading of "Mail Boxes," "Mail Services," or "Telephone Answering Services" (telephone answering services often provide mail forwarding facilities!) one should find a number of firms that provide the type of service needed. The desired service should include receiving, repackaging, and forwarding.

A yellow page directory from any city in the country may be purchased by contacting the local telephone company and requesting the US West Direct yellow page directory distribution point. The charge varies from approximately $5.00 to $30.00, depending on the size of the item. Some public libraries maintain a large selection of the nation's yellow pages directories. If available, this could be an excellent source for research.

In addition to the yellow pages, a book entitled "Directory Of Mail Drops In The United States and Canada," is available from Loompanics Unlimited, P.O. Box 1197, Port Townsend, Wa 98368, price $7. 00. This book contains over 1200 listings, with some overseas listings also provided.

Make it a point to use only a mail forwarding service that offers the use of a street address rather than just a box number. Most of the more sophisticated services offer this because it adds a sense of permanence and respectability.

Be aware that some State and Federal Agencies will not forward important documents to a box number. A street address therefore is essential.

Don't ever consider the U.S. Post Office as a possibility for a mail drop! Even though most post offices do rent mail boxes at a reasonable monthly rate, unnecessary risks are involved. Since the post office is part of the Federal bureaucracy, they are bound to cooperate with other Federal Agencies. Your privacy could easily be invaded. In addition, the post office does not offer the type of remailing services necessary. At the present time, practically all U.S. Post Offices require the prospective box renter to provide ID. This aspect too is undesirable and must be avoided.

If possible, the arrangements for establishing a mail handling service should be made over the telephone or by mail, not in person. A contact could handle this job. A few mail services may request personal ID prior to providing service. By informing the mail service personnel that the call is from out of State, this request is usually forgotten. For those who insist, self-generated documents are usually used. The mailing service may also request a separate billing address. To ensure privacy, the box renter never leaves any pointer or paper trail to his residence. The contact's home address, or even that of another mail drop is often used for this purpose. There are many variations of the maildrop system which can be most effective in protecting one's privacy. The most common one by which a man in the shadows and his contact may communicate is the "single-source" mail drop. In this method, the mail drop (pick-up only) is usually located near the contact's home, and is used for the exclusive purpose of receiving mail only. The desired effect is to protect the contact's home mail box from unwanted intruders.

Another system that works well is the "remote mail drop." In this variation, the mail drop is located in a remote city. Both parties then use the double envelope mailing method to communicate with one another. The third method is the "dual mail drop" and is very popular and by far the most secure. In this system, both parties maintain separate mail drops near their homes. They each send mail to the other's mail drop. Some have devised elaborate chains of maildrops, even utilizing overseas locations in order to ensure privacy.

If a fleeing father wants to maintain mail communication with his children, he can utilize his contact and the mail drop system. All communications can be handled by the contact using the double envelope method. The contact, upon receiving such mail from the father can open the outer envelope and remail the inner envelope(s) to the children, thus protecting the father's home city and state (via the post mark). For obvious reasons, a return address on the inner envelope is changed or omitted.

The children can reply by sending their mail to the contact for remailing. This system may bring heat on the contact if the letter exchange is reported to the Social Services, for it reveals the name and address of the contact. The investigator will likely attempt to turn the contact into an informer. Because of these dangers, a father's communication with his children is safer with one-way mail, or from a remote, preferably out-of-State, pay telephone.

The contact is cautioned against sending mail intended for the man in the shadows from his/her residence. As previously mentioned, the investigator is not above snooping through the contents of a mail box. Mail should be sent from one of the public boxes or a post office. Those residing in the shadows never refer to the new address by name, or the new place of employment in correspondence, even though it is handled through a mail drop. In the unlikely event that the mail drop system becomes contaminated, one does not want to leave tracing information. Mail drop systems, if exposed, can be broken by the courts and various law enforcement agencies. This involves court orders, warrants etc. All seized information then becomes an open book.

Moving And Storing Personal Possessions

Moving personal belongings from a pre-fade address is much more crucial than most people imagine. Do not hint to trusted friends or even relations that a move is near. Nothing prompts an exwife into legal action quicker than the thought of a meal ticket leaving town.

Arranging for a proper moving van (if needed) requires some forethought. Nothing draws more attention and curiosity than a big, noisy, eighteen wheeler with advertisments painted all over its sides pulling up in front of a residence. No matter how careful one has been in planning a departure, an error in judgment such as this could destroy the entire effort. Be assured that the investigator will question neighbors in the area in hopes of finding an informer. All the investigator needs is the name of the carrier who moved the belongings.

If at all possible, make the move in an unmarked truck. Many of the lesser-known movers use unmarked vehicles. These are usually located in the classified section of the newspaper. A rental trailer can also be used to move the household effects to a temporary storage location. Later on, arrangements can be made for a different mover. Curious neighbors will usually inquire where the move is headed. Have a convincing cover prepared for such events.

When utilities are disconnected (phone, gas, lights, etc.) pay them off with cash immediately. If this is impossible, have the final bills forwarded to a mail drop. A contact could also be used to forward payment. Don't leave town with unpaid bills. To do so will only generate additional, and possibly successful, tracing efforts.

Choosing A New Location

In choosing a secure location for building a new life, familiar surroundings must be avoided like the plague. Avoid areas where there are friends, relatives, or even past acquaintances. Those places where one has expressed a desire to reside, or even a favorite vacation spot, must be considered off limits. The reasoning for these precautions is basic, and has been proven sound many times in the past. Those on the run invaribly head for "familliar ground." The news media abounds with stories of wanted individuals apprehended near home and family, or close to relatives or friends.

The selection of a new home should cross one or more state boundaries. Even though distance does not guarantee added security, it does pose additional obstacles to a pursuer and adds a significant amount of time and expense to the search. If the pursuing Social Services Agency is suffering from budget cuts as many are, this ploy might very well discourage additional attempts in the search.

Do not consider living in a small town or a city with a population of less than ten thousand. The citizens of such locations generally pride themselves with being friendly and out-going. This might prompt unwanted interest in the fading individual and his life.

The Right Living Quarters

The selection of proper living quarters in the new location presents no serious obstacles to the man entering a fade. However, several minor precautions should be observed. It has become common practice in many parts of the country to require a prospective renter to fill out a detailed rental agreement prior to moving in. This is generally true in the new and larger, commercially operated apartment complexes. These forms frequently ask for information not in the best interest of those desiring privacy to answer. In addition, most of the rental agreement forms require that personal, and/or rental references be given. Some rental agreement forms even require the name, address and phone number of an employer, including the proposed renter's salary. The professionally managed apartment complexes routinely verify most of the data.

These problems can be overcome by creating the proper cover and utilizing mail drops to receive any inquiries. The replies can be self-generated on appropriate letterhead. However, there are other alternatives that are probably better. In selecting a proper rental unit, focus attention on the small, private owner. The private owner seldom requests written, personal information. The landlord may inquire about sensitive personal matters, but these situations are easily handled by someone properly prepared. Many private owners also agree to having the utilities in their name. This could be a big advantage.

Getting the utilities under one's name without proper ID can present minor problems in some areas of the country. Under no condition does one use a real name or Social Security number on applications submitted to utility companies. The ID obtained under the temporary fade should be sufficient to handle these details.

Telephone service presents some problems of its own. As mentioned before, do not attempt to have a telephone listed under your real name. Even unlisted numbers provide absolutely no privacy whatsoever to the user! "Number tracing" presents a real threat to telephone users who value their privacy. Involved is a small, compact electronic device which is quickly and easily attached to any individual line. This is usually done right on the telephone company's property, and is obvious to no one. The device records and stores any and all incoming phone numbers attempting to access the guarded line. Since conversations are not recorded, and only the calling number is stored, privacy rights have not been violated.

It has been reported that some investigators make wide use of number tracing in order to locate those living under the protective shield of a fade. Placing the device on the suspected lines of mothers, children, relatives, friends, or even a suspected contact, this often provides the investigator with the desired results. Many absent fathers have unknowningly revealed their location simply by calling their children from their home phone. As difficult as it may seem, the use of a totally alien phone, preferably out of state, is advisable under the circumstances.

Applying For A New Job

As in all other aspects of effecting a successful fade, applying for a new job requires advance planning. Whatever fading process (temporary, partial, or complete) is used, the procedure in applying for a new job is similar. In all three methods a different or altered name and Social Security number are essential.

The major concerns for those entering into a fade are how to carry forward work experience from the past to the newely adopted name without leaving a paper trail. Most prospective employers never check with previous employers for references, but there are always the few who do. This is effectivly solved by generating references and previous employment history on self designed letter head. Most any print shop will supply whatever needs there are. A remote mail drop is set up to receive and answer inquiries.

To bypass the possibility of the new employer phoning for prior employment information, inform him/her early in the interview that the firm in question is no longer in business or has gone bankrupt, and that that is the very reason for looking for new employment. If the potential new boss insists on talking on the phone with a reference, the contact could be schooled for this purpose. If added realism is required, bankruptcy cases in the desired area could be checked out. Choose one tailored to fit the needs of the situation, and weave these additional facts into the cover story.

Forged And Counterfeit Documents

Forged ID is the art of using existing documents and altering some or all of the data to correspond to a desired finished product. Forgeries do not stand up under investigation because they do not match the original records. Alterations on many state issued ID cards and drivers licenses are easily detected by law enforcment agencies, especially those that use the Polaroid, or Dec/electro type of process. Some states like California and Florida have special laminations embedded within the paper. An examination under black light will likely reveal any attempts to alter the data on the face of the license or state ID card.

Many commercial establishments, in order to extend credit or open a new account, will ask for a drivers license or ID card. The clerk will then make an examination under black light to check for alterations or forgeries. Needless to say, forgeries are not to be considered as reliable, and are used mainly by amateurs.

Counterfeiting is the science of recreating the entire document with whatever data one desires. Any document created can accurately be duplicated. In the past, the accuracy of the result was dependent upon human skills and knowledge. With the technical advances in materials and methods of today, even an amateur can create acceptable new documents.

An excellent source for full color certificates of all types is Goes Lithographing Co., 42 West 61st St., Chicago, Ill. 60621. 312-684-6700. Goes is the manufacturer, and does not supply them directly, but will give the name of the closest distributor. These certificates are of the highest quality, but are only blanks with colored borders. After the forms are obtained, it will be necessary to retain the services of a printer, or to complete the certificates one's self. See "Self Generated Documents" in a later section of this book.

If in the market for ready-made blank certificates such as birth, baptismal, high school, college, marriage, divorce, etc., etc., contact, Ideal Studios, Box 41156 Chicago, Ill. 60641, telephone number 312-282-9499. A book entitled "ID For Sale," price, $9.95 is available from Loompanics Unlimited, P.O. Box 1197, Port Townsend, WA 98368. This is a catalog of available mail order ID. Additional sources for mail order ID supplies can be located in the classified sections of magazines and newspapers such as the National Inquirer, Star, Globe, Popular Mechanics, Mechanics Illustrated, etc.

The accepted form of validation for most legitimately issued documents is referred to as the "raised" or "impressed" data, created by the seal of the agency in authority. This is called "embossing." This form of validation is accomplished using a "seal die," generally made of a lead/tin alloy, and varing in diameter from one to two inches, the most popular size being the 1 5/8" size. This is the same method used by a Notary Public when validating a signature or date on a document. Corporations and businesses also make wide use of the seal method of validation.

When most States issue a vital statistics record (certificate), the raised validation (embossed data) of the issuing Agency can be found somewhere on the document. Practically all Government Agencies, be it Local, State, or Federal require evidence of this seal before the document is considered certified. In addition to the seal, most agencies also employ the use of a rubber stamp. This stamp usually identifies the issuing agency along with the date and signature of an agency officer.

As incredible as it may seem, the data created by such seals is difficult to read even under the best of conditions. On older documents, the embossed data invaribly becomes flattened out and is virtually impossible to decipher. Most State or Federal agencies (passport agents excepted), will simply "feel" for the raised data with the finger tips to verify its presence, and forgo any attempts to actually read it.

One can obtain self designed seals by consulting the yellow pages under "Stamps and Seals." An abundance of information should be available. One of the best sources is Justrite Stamp and Seal Company, 1301 Grand Ave. Kansas, City Mo., 64106, 816-421-5010. Anyone interested should also obtain a copy of the Salt Lake Stamp Company catalog. This is available by contacting them at 380 West 200 South, P.O. Box 2399 Salt Lake City, Utah, 84110, 801-364-3200.

The Salt Lake Stamp Company handles an abundance of items that may be of interest. In addition to most any kind of rubber stamp imaginable, they also manufacture custom seals to order. In addition, they stock a complete line of embossing labels and tags as used by many agencies for validation purposes. Items of additional interest are their fine selection of employee ID badges, and a large inventory of beautifully made law enforcement badges.

To obtain an exact duplicate of an official State Seal may not be as difficult as one might imagine. Even though a few seal manufacturers may not reproduce an official replica on demand, (there are many exceptions!) they will unknowingly cooperate with the proper request. Most all State Seals are divided into two sections. The inner portion is the actual graphic representation of the State emblem. This is usually a depiction of the State symbol such as the state's outline, or maybe an animal or bird such as a bear, eagle, etc. The outer section (ring) generally specifies an agency name such as, "State of Arizona Department of Health" etc. Such seals are often duplicated by combining two separate seals. By ordering the inner portion from one manufacturer, and the outer ring with a blank center from another, one accomplishes identical results. By selectivly removing unwanted data, a usable impression can be created by using a combination of the two.

It was recently reported that a particular individual devised a very unique method of actually obtaining an official State seal. He set up a mail drop in a medium-sized city in his targeted state. His next step was to have some official looking state letterhead printed. He used a fictitious, nonexistent bureau on the letterhead, listing a mail drop as a return address. He then requested price quotes from a number of out of state seal manufacturers. He also requested samples of their work, and supplied a copy of the desired state seal. The request was signed and stamped as "Assistant Purchasing Agent." Two of the manufacturers actually returned samples of official State Seals designed around the drawing to the mail drop address.

To get an actual imprint of the embossed data from a particular State Seal, simply request a certified copy of a birth certificate, marriage license, or death certificate. For a printed sample, a return letter from the department of interest should provide a good copy.

An official drawing, often in full color, on any of the various State Seals may be obtained by contacting the appropriate Secretary of State's office. Since most official State Seals, emblems, symbols, etc., are approved by the Legislature, official drawings should be available. There are groups of collectors (numismatists) who actually collect samples of State Seals and emblems as a hobby.

Self-Generated Documents

Self-genenerated documents are in many ways superior to the mail-order type. Purchased documents are not as secure as the home-made version for obvious reasons of safety and security, ("someone else knows"). Recent reports allege that some Federal and State Agencies maintain up-to-date samples of mail-order document reproductions. This is especially true of the various State Agencies which issue Drivers Licenses, mostly because of the crack-down on drivers with revoked licenses (driving under the influence of alcohol) attempting to get drivers licenses with phony documents. It has also been reported that many of the commercial establishments engaged in document sales are under constant surveillance by law enforcement agencies, with incoming and outgoing mail being monitored and recorded.

The quality of self-made documents depends mostly on the equipment and materials used, rather than the skill of the individual. There are numerous reports of excellent results being obtained by people with no prior experience. Since State-issued vital statistics documents (birth, death, marriage, divorce, etc.) are only copies of the original, the self-generated type utilizes the same copy methods.

The first document created is generally the birth certificate. This is accomplished in two ways. The first method is to obtain a non-certified copy of one's own birth certificate. The non-certified copy is essential, so that the embossed data will not show up on the newly generated copy. The birth certificate is then taken to a print shop and reproduced minus the typed data. Most printers will comply with this request with no questions asked. For those that do, they are assured that the reproduction is for family genealogy records.

The second method is a total recreation of a generic birth certificate. These are reported to be as good as the originals used by most hospitals.

The birth certificate is laid out on oversized white card stock (posterboard), using black "transfer letters" of the proper point size. The size of the posterboard used is dependent on the camera size used by the print shop engaged to finish the work. The larger the original, the more accurate will be the reduced final copy.

The transfer letters, along with borders, underlines, etc. are available in every size and style imaginable from art or drafting supply firms.

After the over-size birth certificate is complete, it is taken to a copy or print shop to be photo-copied and then reduced to the desired size. Any number of originals can then be produced. The process is known as "Offset." The necessary data is then typed in, and the results recopied on a common copy machine. The product is then ready for the embossing data.

The next item created is usually a colored "photo employee ID card" or "badge." A black and white card may be generated using the same techniques as the birth certificate, but the results are not considered as satisfactory since most employee ID cards are in color. Colored passport style photos are used along with colored transfer letters, underlines, and borders. The system most used for this purpose is called, I.N.T., as in PR<u>INT</u>., manufactured by the 3M Company. It transfers colors in red, blue, green and yellow to almost any surface. The I.N.T. kit is available from most art or drafting supply firms.

After the blank card is fabricated and the data is typed in, the photo is placed in an area previously provided. The card is then laminated in plastic. Lamination kits are available from art or drafting supply houses. The company name used on the ID card is usually fictitious, as is the address. The ID card may be stiffened by attaching it to card stock prior to laminating. For added realism, a message on the back has an "If Found Return To" message.

An alternate method for producing small color ID cards, documents, etc., is by using a Polaroid camera with a close-up lens attachment and an artificial light source. The results are claimed as being good.

The "Reflex" method produces excellent results, too. No camera is required, and absolute privacy is assured because no outside assistance is required. The equipment, materials, and instructions are available from any quality photographic supply house.

Documents created by any of these procedures are not used for purposes that would entail verification, such as passports, Social Security cards, in-State drivers licenses, etc. They have been reported effective in obtaining out-of-State drivers licenses, out-of-State ID cards, or to establish ID for non-Federal employment.

A Word About Computers

This is not a technical review of computers, just a few hints that might enhance one's fading effort. If one understands some of the features and limitations of the computer, the individual might feel more relaxed and confident after the fade is complete.

Most laymen think that computers possess many magical and amazing capabilities. Those who are familiar with the computer and its operation are acutely aware of its many limitations. Computers may be programmed to complete a variety of complex functions. To any man contemplating a fade, the function of "rapid data retrieval" and its variations should be the main point of interest. All personal data (files) stored in a computer's storage devices (disks, tape, etc.) were originally entered by human hand. Any information on a drivers license, automobile registration, or Social Security record(s) was originally obtained from some written record(s). It was necessary for a data entry clerk to enter this information one letter at a time from a computer terminal. Under no conditions is a computer capable of originating or generating this data independently.

If, for example, an individual changed or altered his name and neglected to inform the Department of Motor Vehicles, the Department of Motor Vehicles' computers would never know of the change. Consequently, any time the computer accesses his drivers license number, the original name shows up. If an incorrect address of a mail drop has been supplied to a bank, the bank's computers would have no way of determining the correct address. The point being stressed is, SECRETS ARE EASILY KEPT FROM A COMPUTER.

The one variation of data retrival that must be understood is referred to as the "wild card" option (WCO). It is the WCO that enables the terminal operator (IRS, Department of Motor Vehicles, Social Services Investigator, etc.) several advantages in locating those living underground.

As an example, take the name David R. Johnston, and the Social Security number 408-46-2231. Assume this individual moved across

State lines, changed jobs, and altered the spelling of his last name to Johnson, but retained his original Social Security number. Assuming a search had been initiated, an IRS terminal operator attempting to access any tax files under the original name would see only old data, (address, employer etc). If however, the operator suspected a minor name alteration, he/she could then invoke the WCO. The command given the computer might look sometheng like: $ search D?.R?.J?..

This would be a command for the computer to search its data banks for any names using the initials D.R.J. The operator would get a display showing, among others, the names of Dave R. Johnson, also David R. Johnston, and etc..

Since the original Social Security number was not altered, the original number matches the altered name.

From this data, the IRS would have in their possession the altered name being used, the location of the new employer by means of the the unaltered Social Security number. The IRS investigation would indicate that a David R. Johnston is using the alias of David R. Johnson. This information would be passed on to the State Social Services investigator.

In actuality, the terminal operator would probably not bother with a name on initial attempts to locate a particular individual, but since most Americans are serialized via the Social Security number, this would be the primary means used.

As another example, assume that the same name was modified to Dave C. Johnson. It can readily be seen that the computer would be unable to effectively invoke the WCO because the three initials D.C.-J. are different from the name used in the first case.

However, if the last name just happened to be Jankowski in place of Johnston or Johnson, the uniqueness of the name itself would make the search much easier for the operator. The operator would simply command the computer to display tax files on any persons using the name Jankowski.

Regardless of how the name is altered, unless the Social Security number is also changed, a modified identity will sooner or later be discovered. To modify a Social Security number, similar rules apply. If the last two digits of the Social Security number 408-46-2231 are modified to, say, 408-46-2262, the WCO could be very efficient. A typical command might be: $ search 408-46-22?.?. The computer could then display tax histories of all files from 408-46-2200 thru 408-46-2299. This would involve only 100 files to look through. If the name of Dave C. Johnson was associated with one of the altered numbers, suspicion would arise. The point made should be well established by now: do not overlook the dangers of the WCO when generating a new name, and/or Social Security number. Social Security numbers have a code for generation. This can be found under the Appendix "Social Security Cards."

"Computer networking," is a term well worth remembering. Networking essentially ties together a series of computers through data lines such as telephone lines and associated hardware (modems). This arrangement enables one computer to share data with another (you show me yours, I'll show you mine). All that's necessary for one computer to talk to another is a data line number (phone number) and a password.

Even though it sounds convenient to access another computer's data base, it is often impossible. State and Federal Agencies are very protective about what data is given out. There exists a lot of protectionism and secrecy between bureaucracies. The one major exception is the shared data between the various States and Departments of Motor Vehicles via the "National Drivers Register" (NDR).

Drivers license data and automobile registration information are available from this Federal Agency. A Highway Patrolmen in Florida can avail himself of information on a vehicle or drivers' license from California in a matter of seconds. See the Appendix for additional information on the NDR.

CHAPTER 4

DURING THE FADE

1. Overview
2. Employment
3. Banking
4. Paying reduced amounts of child support
5. An enemy within (IRS)
6. Paying Income Tax
7. Habits

The Overview

After a man initially enters a fade, there are several functions that must be taken into consideration. These are essential procedures necessary to maintaining a successful disappearance over an extended period of time. The subjects covered in this section would apply to all three fading methods.

Employment

Employment and the Social Security number go hand in hand. The investigator places the highest priority on locating the employer of any man who owes past due child support or alimony. It is far more important to locate the place of employment than it is to actually find the man himself who now lives in the shadows. After all, it's really MONEY they want, not the individual. What value is there to a man without money? Would the Social Services investigator be interested in locating a particular male if he was worthless and living in poverty?

The motivation behind the investigator's quest to locate the employer is, of course, salary and whatever additional assets might be revealed. Once the employer has been located, the next step is to legally maneuver to attach any available assets, plus the garnishment of any future salary.

Should either of these actions be carried out, the opportunity to defend one's self in court becomes available, but the options would be extremely limited. The services of a good attorney are essential in this type of situation. For a man in the shadows to become entangled in such circumstances would be disastrous, to say the least. The "ball game" would be over, and the tedious prospects of going into another fade could very well become reality.

Every employer in the country is required by law to obtain a Federal Tax Identification number. In addition, most States require that employers obtain a State Tax Identification number. When an employer files these tax statements, (usually quarterly), they must show the amounts of taxes and Social Security insurance withheld from each employee. To identify who paid how much, the individual's Social Security number is used on the employer's quarterly tax forms. This is the very reason for the careful generation of a new Social Security number. This is also the reason never to compromise one's place of employment. Because of these dangers, it is much more secure if a contact is not informed of the new employer.

This is one area where extreme caution is absolutely essential. If the place of employment has been revealed, the individual becomes secondary. Consider the store of information that the investigator can gather from such a source! The name presently being used, the new Social Security number, payroll savings if any, (don't be foolish here!), the name and address of banking facilities, etc. (see section on Banking).

As additional precautionary measures, never use any type of an employee savings plan such as a credit union, savings bonds, stock plans, etc. The reasoning is, if accidentally located, it becomes a simple matter for some meddling bureaucrat to gain control of such assets. This is usually done very quickly and without the owner's prior knowledge.

Just nother example of how free we actually are.

Banking

After entering a fade it may be desirable to establish secure banking services. It is advisable that the establishment where payroll checks are cashed be kept seperate from the bank one actually does business with (savings, checking, etc.). The best institution for cashing a payroll check could be a supermarket or other public exchange. The bank where the payroll check is drawn on is another possibility. One banking institution is used solely for the purpose of cashing payroll checks. The second institution will be used for depositing cash only. Neither institution is made aware of the other. This procedure is referred to as the "dual banking system."

What is the reasoning behind this extra effort? If one living in a fade is accidentally located and he has made the mistake of using only one bank for cashing and depositing, cancelled payroll checks will be a perfect pointer to his employer and other possible assets.

Banks and lending institutions are an arm of Federal or State bureaucracies and will cooperate in any attempt to locate a man in the shadows. The Social Security number, name, or any other personal data could be used to establish ownership of assets. Fortunately, banks very seldom, if ever, require one to show a Social Security card. They simply request your number. To camouflage assets could be accomplished by generating a second fictitious name and Social Security number, and then open a seperate account.

All banks require some form of identification prior to opening an account. The bank one chooses to do business with will likely request information on the place of employment. It would be a grave error to provide correct information here! Instead, the alert man in the fade gives them the personal and employment information he wants them to have, his "new" version. Some employment possibilities are: freelance photographer, writer, self-employed salesman, construction worker, etc. Give only employment information that is difficult, if not impossible, to verify.

It is most desirable that the bank not know of one's real residence address. This can easily be accomplished by the use of a mail drop address in order to receive correspondence from the bank such as cancelled checks, statements, etc. If personalized checks are used, a mail drop address is also ideal in lieu of one's actual address.

The commercial banking industry in the United States is totally dominated by the Federal Government. Hence, the IRS has assumed a tyrannical watchdog role over the bank's depositors.

Beware of any bank or savings institution if concerned about financial secrecy, personal privacy, or most of all, safety. For those interested in offshore banking, a book titled "Using An Offshore Bank For Profit, Privacy And Tax Protection" by Jerome Schneider is available from WFI Publishing Corporation, 2049 Century Park East, Los Angeles, CA., 213-553-8700. Another excellent book on the subject is titled, "Mark Skowsen's Complete Guide To Financial Privacy," ($17.95) available from Phillips Publishing, Inc., 7811 Montrose Road, Potomac, Maryland 20854.

Be aware that any bank, as a matter of course, forwards to the IRS records of all interest paid on savings or checking on a yearly basis. If a checking account must be established, it is beneficial to choose a bank that pays no interest.

If living in a fade, it is imperative to NEVER, ABSOLUTELY NEVER, maintain large amounts (more than one can afford to lose) of cash in any bank-, savings-, or checking account, or even in a safety deposit box. The IRS can and will confiscate and/or attach these assets without court permission or even the owner's prior knowledge. The IRS, with full cooperation of the bank, monitors targeted accounts for extended periods of time, waiting for a higher-than-normal account balance before striking. In spite of what one may have heard, there is no buffer or isolation between one's assets and the greedy, long arm of the Federal Government.

The IRS is unusually adept at the brazen, and unconstitutional practice of seizing a citizen's assets without notification, thereby ignoring the due process of law. Redress will take place only after the assets have been confiscated. The burden of proving rightful ownership to such assets will lie totally with the account owner. Abuses such as these make a truly free society seem like a fantasy of the past.

To ensure at least semi- financial privacy and reduce the risks of commercial banking, money orders and certified checks should be considered. They are very difficult to trace and leave fewer distinct paper trails.

Paying Reduced Amounts Of Child Support

How does a father living in a fade pay child support (the amount he can actually afford), without being detected? If he should mistakenly send support payments on one of his own checks (it has happened before!) his ex-wife will have him at her disposal within days. Even an envelope bearing a revealing post mark can lead to unwanted intrusion of one's privacy. Your contact is a valuable assistance in these matters.

Send a money order to the contact's mail drop. A fictitious name is used on the money order for added protection. The contact then deposits the money order in his/her own account and purchases a second money order. This second money order will show the father's correct name, but needs no return address for added security. It will then be forwarded, by the contact, to the proper State Agency for recording. If no contact is used, the "double envelope" mail drop system can be used.

The investigator will be watching any child support transactions very closely for postmarks or any other type of forgetfulness. As an added precaution and for one's own protection, always send child support payments to the proper Agency, not the ex-wife directly. Most States have made provisions to accept child support payments through an Agency such as the County Recorder, etc. This provides the most secure method of ensuring that one actually receives credit for payments made. Ex-wifes have been known to distort the truth when it comes to the actual amount of child support they are receiving.

Many absentee fathers are paying less child support than the Court ordered. Under these circumstances it is imperative that he or his contact clearly mark on the face of each support payment the month and year the payment is for. Make sure to maintain a copy for permanent records. If this detail is neglected, waiting out the statute of limitations might prove useless. A clever attorney for the plaintiff could possibly claim that all amounts paid were actually being paid on past due obligations, not current ones. The dollar difference could be staggering.

An Enemy Within (IRS)

The Internal Revenue Service as it exists today, must certainly be classified as the single biggest threat to the Constitution. The main point of contention between freedom-loving individuals and the IRS is the absence of fair and unbiased treatment when accused of a tax violation. The IRS has the judicial power to completely eliminate the due process of law. When a tax dispute does exist between the private taxpayer and the IRS, the IRS presides over the matter and invariably makes rulings in favor of itself. The only solution to this type of treatment is to acquire the aid of a tax attorney and appeal to the Federal Tax Court system. Of course, this usually costs more than paying the taxes themselves would.

Most of the derogatory adjectives associated with the IRS appear to be well earned. This exemplifies only a small portion of the negative feelings from the tax payer. Decent people generally view the IRS as an equivalent to the Nazi Gestapo of World War II. Because the reputation of the IRS is held in such low esteem, truly capable people refuse to consider the IRS as a viable place in which to build their career.

Because of this, the IRS seems to attract an unusually high percentage of unscrupulous individuals, unqualified, and undertrained who frequently engage in activities that are morally unacceptable, such as prevarication (lying), illegal seizures (stealing), deception (cheating), and physical brutality. There are numerous reports of taxpayers who have been seriously injured, even killed, by Federal Agents in their zeal to seize private assets by force.

Most errors committed by IRS employees stem from the fact that they do not know the tax laws sufficiently to aid the taxpayer or solve tax problems lawfully. Since the IRS has rightfully earned such a despicable reputation for underhanded and dishonest dealings with the public, very few taxpayers voluntarily comply 100% with the standards issued by the IRS.

The dollar losses incured by the US Treasurey because of such IRS inequities must be monumental!

A man living under the disguise of a fade must be prepared to interface with the IRS. He may be using a new name and an altered Social Security number. This will cause a mismatch between the name and the Social Security number in the IRS computer data banks. As mentioned previously, this type of error is common, and happens many thousands of times each year. The IRS may send the individual or his employer Federal form 3912 for verification. If questioned by one's employer, identical data is re-submitted. The employer will then reply (many employers never reply) with the same data. If the form is sent to an individual, it is usually ignored. The IRS sends these forms out by the hundreds of thousands, and it is normal to receive only a small percentage of replies.

The Department of Social Services depends heavily on financial support and programs devised by the Department of Health, Education and Welfare (HEW). "GOTCHA" is one such program.

It was devised by Federal bureaucrats to seize tax refunds of those men who are behind in child support and/or alimony obligations.

The Gotcha scheme claims to be searching for "absent parents," but the obvious intent is to persecute and financially injure divorced men. By being part of such discriminatory despotism, the Federal Government has lowered and degraded itself to the position of a civil bill collector. This for the sole benefit of inactive, lazy, unskilled, and non-productive women.

The principal means of location used in this program is the name and Social Security number as they appear on Federal tax returns.

Most men living in a fade have effected a name change, modified their Social Security number, and have insulated themselves against such action. Most are aware of the dangers involved in over-paying State or Federal income taxes. They do not permit the Government to confiscate hard-earned money by foolishly overpaying during the tax year. Why provide an interest-free loan to such an unappreciative borrower?

During the tax year, be aware of the precautions required for the protection of personal privacy. When estimating exemptions for tax purposes, always arrange estimated payroll tax deductions to remain just slightly behind amounts actually due. Never allow the IRS to end up with any type of an appreciable surplus. A good CPA can estimate income and deductions to accomplish the desired results.

As additional insurance, enclose a slight overpayment when submiting the return(s); $25.00 is usually sufficient. The reason for this is to create a small windfall for the IRS. The typical IRS agent will be prompted by his/her basic greed to confiscate the overpayment because of the existing mismatch between name and Social Security number. Any motivation for locating the errant tax payer will be greatly diminished because of the small overage they then appropriate.

Beware of a favorite tactic reportedly used by the IRS and State Tax collectors referred to as "reverse baiting." This scheme is resorted to when the IRS is on the trail of a man suspected of living in the shadows. The IRS will send (to the last known address, or even the address of a contact) a small check that appears to be a tax refund. The tax agent then patiently waits for the suspect to cash the check. If things go according to plan, the agent will soon have what he has been waiting for: the name and location of the suspect's bank. This could reveal the employer or other assets.

Men residing in a fade are alert to the dangers involved in this form of trickery and react accordingly. It's a simple matter for most males to defuse a situation like this. They endorse the check with the name as shown, and cash the check at a public exchange, never in their own account. An alternate solution is to use the dual banking system, or even an overseas bank, in order to give the IRS agent a real workout.

It has recently been reported but not verified, that the IRS has issued some secretly marked checks in its reverse baiting program. The purpose of the marking is to alert banking personnel to "fish" for additional information, address, employer, etc.

Paying Income Tax

A man living in either a temporary or partial fade will file his Federal and State income taxes with several minor modifications (the complete fade has a seperate method). If the name, and/or Social Security number has been altered, any connection between the correct name, Social Security number, and the new employer, are not divulged. To do so would expose the fade in its entirety. Privacy is maintained by filling out the tax forms as always, but using the real name, correct Social Security number, and omiting a return address. When sending it in, simply leaving out the W2 form supplied by the employer completes the procedure. The W2 form could be altered by deleting the employer's name, address and ID number, but to simply leave it out will be an explainable omission later on. When received by the IRS, it will appear as if the correct individual actually filed the return, but erroneously neglected to enclose the W2 form. This is a common mistake committed by thousands of taxpayers each year. If desired, substituting the address of a distant mail drop could help confuse location efforts. The object is to break any link or connection between the adopted name, altered Social Security number, and the real ones. The new employer also remains unidentified on the tax forms.

Habits

Changing habit patterns is essential to success when in a fade. If an established habit pattern has become predictable, it must be altered. If a man entering a fade has been devoted to a fraternal order such as Elks, Moose, etc., a change in life style is essential. It would be the same for any social or religious affiliation. An attachment for a particular labor union would hold the same risks.

Many men successfully living under the protective cover of a fade have accepted new lifestyles and met new and exciting people. Most claim they have never been happier.

CHAPTER 5

THE TEMPORARY FADE

1. The Overview
2. Changing Your Name
3. Temporary ID
4. The Department of Motor Vehicles
5. Closing The Door

The Overview

The temporary fade is used primarily for delaying tactics and for short periods of time, lasting usually a year or less. If the time element is critical and immediate action is required, this fade is often the only solution. Some men have extended this method for much longer periods, but this is considered as pressing one's luck. If time periods in excess of a year are required, work is usually started on one of the more permanent procedures.

The principles behind a temporary fade are the use of a different name and altering one's Social Security number. A new job across State lines may also be necessary. In many States, a name change may be accomplished by simply utilizing the "use" method. A person simply adopts whatever name is desired, then notifies the proper agencies, and simply starts using the name. No legal procedures are usually required. The results will be to completely dissapear from old familiar surroundings and start a new life under new and different conditions.

Changing Your Name

American Jurisprudence, Volume 57 states;

"You have a common law right to change your name by simply adopting a new one without legal proceedings, unless there is a specific State statute to the contrary. The one universal exception is that you may not change your name for fraudulent purposes. Maintaining privacy is not considered fraudulent in some states.

This opinion from the State of Massachusetts, shared by both the Attorney General and the Secretary of State dated December 5, 1975 states:

"It has always been the law of this Commonwealth that any individual, male or female, has the right to choose and from time to time change his or her name. This right is not contained in any statute or other codified form. Rather, it is a common law right which the courts have consistently recognized so long as he or she has no intent to defraud anyone by the use of such name.

Although it is common practice for a person wishing to change his or her name to present a petition for change of name, such a court order is not required by law. A person may change his or her name simply by using another name."

The procedures and laws pertaining to a name change vary widely throughout the United States. However, most States abide by the two accepted methods of changing one's name, which are the "court" and the "use" methods.

A temporary fade usually involves a name change utilizing the "use" method. This is by far the quickest. The following is a sample name change form used in adopting a new name. Use only in those States that legally authorize the "use" method.

DECLARATION OF LEGAL NAME CHANGE

I the undersigned, being 18 years of age or older, declare that the forgoing is true and correct:

I,____________________________, born_______________________________
(present name) (name on birth certificate)

in__________________________County, in the State of _______________

on the_________day of_____________ _______________
(Month) (Year)

Do hereby declare my intent to change my legal name, and henceforth be exclusively known as,

____________________________________ _______________________________
(new name) (new signature)

dated______________________________

____________________________________dated__________________________
(notary signature)

The laws of the various States are in a constant state of flux, and may change on a yearly basis. Before executing plans for any type of name change it is essential that the reader investigate the laws for the State of interest. For additional information, see the Appendix on name change.

California's name change laws are ideally suited for those considering a change of name via the "use" method. Hollywood, the center for thousands of actors popularized the practice of assuming stage names by the "use" method years ago. The procedure has since gained acceptance by the general public and is used by thousands of Californians each year to effect an accepted and inexpensive method of changing a name.

Temporary ID

Along with a name change, it may be necessary to accumulate some type of documentation (ID) to make it viable. To obtain official State and Federal documents is not necessary, but will be required under the two other fading techniques (partial and complete). For a complete listing of where to get temporary ID consult the section on "Forged and Counterfeit Documents". If time permits, selfgenerated ID is often of better quality and more secure than the mail-order type. See the section on self-generated documents. However, for the short term, the ID available from mail order houses may be sufficient. Cashing payroll checks will require supporting ID. An employee ID card is usually sufficient. These are usually self-generated. Reference "Self-Generated Documents" in another chapter.

When asked for a Social Security card, very few requestors actually want to see the card but are satisfied with the number recalled from memory. This situation is capitalized on when supplying an altered Social Security number. The code for generating Social Security numbers can be found under the section on that subject. Another possibilty to consider is the temporary Social Security card. The Social Security office will issue temporary cards to individuals who have lost, misplaced, or forgotten the correct number. Check with your Social Security office for details.

In a temporary fade, speed is of the essence. Time may not permit the proper exchanging of ID documents, drivers license, state ID card, etc. One may be forced to use his original drivers license and automobile registration while at the same time using a different name for employment purposes. This could present an impossible situation if a drivers license is a requirement for employment. In situations such as these, it would be necessary to effect one of the more advanced methods of fading.

The Department of Motor Vehicles

As a man entering a temporary fade, obtaining a valid Drivers License and automobile registration will be foremost in his mind. Since this fade is temporary, the original Drivers License is used.

However, if the license is close to expiration, it should be renewed prior to leaving for another location. This will solve the problem of renewing the license at a later date and possibly divulging the new address. Since the Department of Motor Vehicles is a favored information source for the Social Services investigator, leaving paper tracks on a drivers license renewal form is avoided.

Automobile registration is also accomplished through the Department of Motor Vehicles. The same precautions as with a drivers license are used. If necessary, a contact and the mail drop system could be used for obtaining new license plates or a drivers license.

After a fade has been entered, the missing male may have his drivers license or automobile registration "flagged" by computer for updated personal data (latest address, current employer etc.).

This is usually initiated as a request from the Social Services investigator directly to the Department of Motor Vehicles. Any officer who encounters a flagged drivers license or automobile registration will be instructed to obtain the new information. This flagged alert (often called a "hit") is usually received via the officer's two-way radio after the license and registration have been verified by computer. Most men living in a fade are prepared for such tactics. They never reveal their actual employer nor correct residence.

Closing The Door

The final technique is that of setting up a smoke screen, more often referred to as "closing the door. " There are two steps to this procedure. The first is to fill out a change of address card at the local post office. The information given is of course fictitious, such as an address arbitrarily chosen from an out-of-State phone directory or even a mail drop overseas. The purpose is to create a deception for those in pursuit.

The second step of the operation is initiated by simply requesting a copy of one's credit rating. Consulting the yellow page directory under the heading of Credit Bureaus, firms providing such services will be listed. The application fee is about $10.00. Filling out an application for a credit report copy also offers the unique opportunity to generate a fictitous address that is widely accepted and accessible nationwide. Many persecuted males take advantage of this feature by supplying the same fictitious address used on the change of address card. The Social Services investigator will no doubt obtain this information.

CHAPTER 6

THE PARTIAL FADE

1. The Overview
2. Name Change Options
3. Exchanging ID
4. Birth Certificates
5. Drivers Licenses
6. State ID Cards
7. Social Security Numbers

The Overview

The partial fade is just as the name implies, partial. The purpose of this type of anonymity is one of medium duration. Where the use of the temporary fade is not extended beyond one year, the partial fade has been extended considerably longer. Depending on individual circumstances, the partial fade has been used by some for five years or longer.

The security offered by the partial fade depends to a large extent on the care taken during the planning stage and the intensity and financial backing of those searching for him. The partial fade is usually more secure than the temporary fade because of the officially issued ID involved.

The basis of a partial fade involves a name change (using either the "court" or "use" methods) in a State which generates few if any paper trails, and exchanging old ID for new documentation. A modified Social Security number is also required. If one neglects to inform the various State and Federal bureaucracies of the change, he has essentially become invisible to those searching. In a way, computers have become a blessing in disguise to those living in a fade. Many organizations have become so reliant on the computer that human intuition is often bypassed. By merely making a few discreet alterations in a name and a number, a member of the human race in effect "ceases to exist".

Name Change Options

Unless a particular State has laws specifically forbiding the "use" method of a name change, American Jurisprudence, Volume 57 states that this method is legal. California law states that the individual has the right to change his/her name under the usage method (Code of Civil procedures 1279.5 (a)).

In the "court" method it may become necessary to petition the court with an application for a new name. In some States it is required that the services of an attorney be obtained. In addition to attorney fees, a filing fee may be charged. Some States are preferred over others because of the obvious absence of a paper trail. There is a brief summary in the appendices of individual State requirements to effect a name change. As can be seen, the "use" method is by far the more convenient of the two. Most males living in a fade are reported to be using the "use" method because of its simplicity and self-imposed controls. Most also use altered Social Security numbers on name-change applications.

Exchanging ID

After the successful completion of a name change, many simply exchange old documents for a new drivers license, ID card, etc. After arriving in the adopted State, the ID is usually exchanged again. Obtaining a Social Security card is accomplished by obtaining the services of the proper print shop. The section on Social Security cards and the appendix give additional information. Some use self-generated documents to obtain new, fresh ID. Refer to the section on self-generated documents. Some have added extra security to their new identity by exchanging ID in several States following a name change. This seems to be a matter of choice, but could offer increased stumbling blocks to the investigator.

Birth Certificates

If a name change has taken place via the "court" method, the court will issue a document stating such. A new birth certificate <u>will not</u> be issued. The facts are, a name change of any type does <u>not</u> entitle a person to a new birth certificate. Some States will make an attachment to the original birth record showing a name change has taken place. This amounts to undesireable paper tracks that most men in a fade avoid.

Drivers Licenses

Getting a drivers license after a name change without leaving paper tracks is a common problem facing most men entering a partial fade.

The applicant advises the Department of Motor Vehicles that a name change has taken place, and a new drivers license will be sent in the mail. Some States may require that a form be filled out. When last checked, California had no requirements for forms. Women getting married or divorced are constantly changing last names. To reflect these changes on a drivers license or ID card is commonplace. The same holds true for men. Refer to the Appendix on drivers licenses for additional information, specifically the National Drivers Register, (NDR).

State ID Cards

Most States issue ID cards from their Department of Motor Vehicles. Since little emphasis is placed on these cards, very few States share this information. Many men entering a fade will obtain only the ID card after a name change and proceed to a separate State for a drivers license. The newly issued ID card is then used for identification in obtaining the new drivers license.

Social Security Numbers

Practically all males successfully living under the protective umbrella of a fade are using modified Social Security numbers. As previously mentioned, it is very seldom, if ever, that an individual is actually requested to display the card. Simply recalling the number is more than sufficient for most Agencies.

Some divorced males are generating their own Social Security cards (old style only) using the methods outlined in the section on Self-generated Documents. Color copiers have been used, but the results are of poor quality. Some print shops will do the job without asking questions. Excellent counterfeit Social Security cards are also available, but to find a source can be a real problem. Some have reported that these sources are located by contacting illegal workers, usually of Mexican origin. The Department of Social Security has been compromised on occassions, and real Social Security cards with valid numbers have been sold by employees for $1,500.00 and up.

Some persecuted males entering a partial fade have attempted to obtain a new Social Security card by applying directly to the Social Security office. This usually results in failure because as an adult male, they are thoroughly scrutinized as being suspect. Social Security personnel are trained to watch for this type of deception. Most documents, mainly the birth certificate, would be checked out. Those who do succeed are reported to be using self-generated baptismal certificates.

Freedom

CHAPTER 7

THE COMPLETE FADE

1. The Overview
2. The New Birth Certificate
3. Final Preparations
4. The New State ID Card
5. The New Drivers License
6. Supporting ID
7. The New Social Security Card
8. Obtaining A Passport
9. Establishing Credit
10. Keeping A Low Profile

The Overview

In the previous chapters, the temporary and partial methods of fading have been discussed. Both of these arrangements have definite restrictions, mainly that of duration. The temporary fade was designed primarily as a delaying tactic in order to buy precious time for one of the more secure methods of fading. The methods utilized in the temporary fade are not generally extended beyond a year. The partial fade was conceived for men wanting to become anonymous for an intermediate period of time, three to five years maximum.

The time period assigned to a particular type of fade is at best approximate, and could vary greatly depending upon individual circumstances. As an example, consider the case of one individual who managed to expand a temporary fade into an eight-year stint. This particular divorced male periodically and systematically changed employment and Social Security numbers on a yearly basis. In his never-ending quest for financial freedom, he managed new and different schemes to pay both Federal and State income taxes after each job change.

He lived under the constant threat of discovery and became so paranoid that he refused to have a telephone in his residence. He would not even respond to a knock on his door. This type of lifestyle is totally unnecessary and can easily be avoided with the proper technique and planning. Had this particular gentleman known the procedures to effect a more lasting fade, life could have been kinder in all respects.

The complete fade is the absolute epitomy of the art of fading.

This little-known procedure is so effective that the Government is reported to have made numerous attempts to conceal the procedure from the general public. It has been rumored that its use is a well-kept but often-used secret amoung those engaged in undercover spying.

It has been stated that the basics of the complete fade are regularly used by the FBI to relocate and give new identities to underworld figures willing to testify against former associates. Knowledgable underworld figures have successfully utilized the system to become inaccessible for years on end without ever being discovered.

After the sucessful conclusion of a complete fade, one could have in his possession a totally new name and a certified copy of a State-issued birth certificate. It would then be possible to obtain a new and authentic ID card and drivers license. Finally, securing a new Social Security card issued by Uncle Sam's own Agency would complete the transition. For those in need, the procedure to obtain an official passport is discussed in this chapter.

The New Birth Certificate

The unique features involved in a complete fade are centered around the acquisition of a certified copy of a State-issued birth certificate of a person who died before reaching maturity. Once the birth certificate has been obtained, it then becomes a simple matter to build a new set of identification documents around this basic foundation.

At the present time there are in excess of seven thousand local vital statistics record offices (approximately one per county) within the United States. These offices process approximately ten and a half million copies of birth certificates annually, mostly through the mail. The acquisition of a proper birth certificate to fit one's needs should be accomplished through a mail drop system for security reasons.

The person whose identity is under consideration as a namesake would ideally have died as a youngster, not over 12 years of age, preferrably as an infant. Primary interests would be a birth certificate of an individual who died before normally accruing documents of his own such as a Social Security number (with the death of its original owner on file), extensive school or church records, etc.

Starting with a clean background is absolutely necessary. This will enable one to obtain new, untarnished documentation of his own. The birth certificate required will be that of an individual born somewhere around the same year as one's own birthday. To give or take five years is generally acceptable.

As a starting point, some basic research on several outlying States will be required. It is essential to know where to obtain vital statistics records from the selected States. Refer to the Appendix on this subject.

As a precautionary measure, do not obtain the birth certificate of an individual from your own resident State (for obvious security reasons). Even though some States do not cross-reference birth and death records across county lines, the added security of crossing State lines is well worth the time and effort. <u>Under no conditions should the birth certificate of an individual whose birth and death were recorded in the same county, be considered</u>. The birth certificate of a youngster who was born in one State, yet died in another, is essential. What's the reasoning behind all of this precaution? Many States are combining the vital statistics data (remember computer networking?) of their various counties into a cross-referenced data bank. If the birth record of a person whose birth and death occured in the same State is used, the possibility of discovery would be greatly increased. Also, the individual's death may have been recorded on the birth record. Such a birth certificate must be considered worthless and unusable.

At the present time there are no known States cross-referencing birth and death records among one another. However, most States are cooperating with the Social Security office in supplying Social Security numbers of the deceased. Thus, the value of obtaining the birth records of an individual before a Social Security number was ever issued. However, under certain conditions, it can be extremely advantageous to obtain the birth certificate of an individual who was indeed issued a Social Security card prior to his death. These conditions will be covered later in this Chapter under Social Security cards.

There is one type of birth certificate that is considered the prize among prizes to those living on borrowed documents. This rare and most sought-after document is the birth certificate of an individual who died without a death certificate ever being recorded. These are extremely difficult to locate, but do exist in some of the more remote, rural parts of the country. They are usually located by scouring unregistered family grave plots and using grave marker information as a starting point for basic research. It would have to be verified that the individual's birth and death occured in the same local area. This is to preclude the possibility of a death certificate being issued in another County or State.

Another source is the youthful American who died in a country other than the USA, where official word of the death never reached his home. This is a rare occurrence but does happen in some of the more remote, backward countries of the world.

A few persecuted males permanently residing in a complete fade entered the fade via the route of a delayed certificate of birth.

This is accomplished by generating unverifiable support documents such as church baptismal records, family bible records, circumcision records, etc., and applying for a delayed birth record. All States have a procedure to issue a delayed certificate of birth. Those seeking lifelong residency in a complete fade usually desire the extra security offered by this method.

Final Preparations

Shopping for a birth certificate requires a good workable procedure, coupled with careful planning. In most areas, vital statistics records are open to the general public, and "record browsing" is permitted (reference the appendix on where to write for vital statics records). This is especially true in the smaller rural counties. If this is the case, one is free to select a birth certificate nominee at leisure. Simply examine the death records until a likely candidate is located, then request a copy of the individual's birth certificate through the mail.

Many of the larger metropolitan areas such as New York City, Los Angeles, San Francisco, etc., have placed certain restrictions on access to their vital statistics records. Arizona, Washington, Florida and Tennessee, to name a few, have closed their files to "record browsing," but access is always available to those who prepare in advance. These troublesome States have not actually closed the records off from public view, but have placed effective "stumbling blocks" in the way in order to discourage the unprepared.

Some States require that anyone desiring to examine death records fill out a form requesting detailed personal information about the deceased in an effort to discourage "record browsing." In addition, a small charge may be assessed. It is absolutely essential that a call be made prior to an actual visit, in order to be completely prepared well in advance. If there is a requirement that a form be completed, get a copy of the form. If the necessary preparations have been made, virtually all vital statistics departments will be available and open for inspection. Fortunately, some professions command full access to the vital statistics records of even the most restrictive States. These include:

1. Law Enforcement Agencies
2. Private Investigators
3. Attorneys
4. Legimate family members (searching for a family members)
5. Tracers of lost persons
6. Genealogists

Of this list, the most promising prospect is that of the "Genealogist. " Genealogy groups are numerous throughout the country, and most are continually seeking out new members. Membership usually includes the issuance of ID cards, forms, and many other useful items that will prove to be invaluable aids to record browsing.

Self-generated genealogy ID is another possibility worth consideration. Armed with the credentials of a genealogist, one should experience little difficulity in accessing most any State's vital statistics records.

Consulting the yellow pages of any metropolitan city phone directory, under Genealogy, one can find an abundance of information on the services and agencies available. The option of hiring a professional genealogist merits consideration. Most public libraries have a section on the subject, and it would be well worth the time to investigate.

The Salt Lake City, Utah area is an absolute Mecca for the student of genealogy. The LDS Church (Mormons) maintains the largest genealogy data banks in the entire world and they are open to the general public. Record browsing, in fact, is encouraged! It is a well known fact that many State and Federal Agencies (including the FBI) CIA, and IRS among others, freely use the LDS church geneaology data banks for their own less-than-commendable purposes. There are also numerous supply houses located in the city that can supply most any type of genealogy paraphernalia in existance.

It is most advisable that anyone seriously considering genealogical research obtain a recent copy of the Salt Lake City, Utah, yellow page directory. This is an excellent reference source for genealogical materials. To obtain a copy, contact US West at 1-800-243-2960. Some of the larger public libraries often have a stock of the nation's yellow page directories. The telephone companies may offer information on the location of such libraries.

The following publications are an invaluable aid and worthwhile in preparing for the search of a birth certificate candidate.

"Unpuzzling Your Past" By Emilly Anne Croom. Available from Loompanics Unlimited, P.O. Box 1197, Port Townsend, Wa. 98368. The price is $7.95. Also included are over 20 blank forms such as interview forms, sample letters, worksheets, multi-generation forms, etc.

"Where To Write For Birth and Death Records." Available from US Government Printing Office, Washington, D.C. 20402. DHEW publication number HRA 76-1142, stock number 017-022-00486-1, price: 35 cents.

"Where To Write For Marriage Records," DHEW publication number HRA 76-1144, price: 35 cents. Address same as above.

"Where To Write For Divorce Records," DHEW publication number, HRA 76-1145, price: 35 cents. Address same as above.

"How To Trace Your Family Tree" Dolphin Books, Doubleday and Company, Garden City, New York, Price: $2.95.

Actually, the first step in researching for a suitable birth certificate to fit one's needs should not be a visit to the vital statistics records office. In fact, it might not be required at all. The first preliminary research normally takes place at one of the larger newspapers in the targeted State. Most newspapers maintain microfilm libraries of every newspaper they ever published. These libraries are used by the multitudes for just about any type of research imaginable. Call ahead for details. Any legitimate reason is usually sufficient to use the library. As an example, a student writing a research paper on accidental deaths in the area for the years 1937 and 1938 would have valid reasons to use the library. In all probibility, no reasons will be necessary, but have one ready just in case. Genealogy ID could prove useful, too.

Once in the library, the main point of interest will focus on the local pages, and of course, the obituary section. Since the time frame has already been decided (one's own birthday, plus or minus five years), obituary records from these dates is a good starting point. Looking through these columns, locate the record of a youngster or even an infant, who died within the proper time frame. The local pages are also helpful as accidental deaths are often used as feature articles. The name of a newly born infant is not used because a birth certificate may have been issued showing the baby as having been "stillborn."

As previously mentioned, it is absolutely essential that the individual's birth and death occurred in a separate State. This information is usually contained in the obituary writeup. With a little effort, a satisfactory list of five or six names could be completed in a single afternoon. Avoid the use of unusual names, or individuals from uncommon ethnic origins. Do not use the names of descendants from the rich or famous. The less notoriety, the better! Most micro film libraries will make copies of the data desired for a nominal charge. If this service is not available, it will be necessary to hand-copy the data from the obituary. This will be useful in obtaining the actual birth certificate.

From this newspaper research, it is possible to obtain a complete file of data on a chosen namesake. Valuable data such as date of birth, date of death, place of birth, place of death, names of parents, brothers, sisters, and possibly other relatives etc... If additional information is required such as marriage records, divorce records, information on additional relatives, etc., the basic information from which to build is easily obtained. Use the publication list located in this book to gather any other vital statistic record needed.

Building a complete and detailed portfolio on any individual desired becomes possible. As can readily be seen, adequate research will prepare one to access any State's vital statistics records. The obituary research should enable one to fill out any questionaire or form because the necessary data is available.

Before continuing, it is absolutely necessary that a death record be obtained. Newspapers often make errors when preparing a news article or an obituary. First, middle, and last names must be verified for correct spelling, as is all other personal data. Any vital statistics office would be rightly suspicious of a person who misspelled his own name or did not know his correct birthday.

Now is the time to gather whatever additional data is available from the vital statistics records. Obtain any data on the selected list of individuals not previously available. Take this opportunity to further enhance the portfolios. A primary point of interest is whether the death record lists a Social Security number. If the death record shows that a number was issued, this is vitally important information. This could destroy the value of the particular birth certificate, or it could be a very valuable enhancement. The birth certificate would be of little value if a Social Security number was issued and the Social Security office was notified of the death. Fortunately, thousands of Social Security numbers are recorded on the various States' death records, but were never reported to the Department of Social Security. Read the section on Social Security cards later in the chapter.

Take the newly acquired obituary data and request, through the mail, (a mail drop address should be used) copies of the various birth certificates, ideally all from separate States. It would be wise to apply for more than one birth certificate in order to be prepared for a varity of unforseen circumstances. Be cautious if requesting several birth certificates from the same State. If computer networking is invloved, the request may be flagged if the same mailing address is used for more than one birth certificate.

When requesting a copy, the newly adopted name is used on a first person basis. Say, for example, that the chosen namesake is Thomas Larry Smith. A request for a birth certificate using that name might look something like this:

> Dear Sirs:
>
> My name is Thomas Larry Smith. I was born in Peach Tree, Georgia, on May 14, 1952. My Father's name <u>was</u> Henry George Smith, and my Mother's name <u>is</u> Ida May Farnsworth Smith.

Please send me a copy of my birth certificate, which I need for employment purposes. I have enclosed a money order for $8.00 to cover expenses.

Sincerely,

Tom Smith

This sample letter contains all the information a Department of Vital Statistics Office would normally require. Father's full name, mother's maiden name, place and date of birth, and relationship (self) of the applicant to owner of the birth record. Also note the indication that the father had passed away (was) and the mother is still living (is). This places an additional enhancement on the request.

Within several weeks, the birth certificate copies should start arriving at the designated mail drop. From the list of birth certificates, select the one that looks best. Thoroughly study the portfolio created on the chosen candidate. Important dates, names and places should be committed to memory. Nothing will destroy a fade faster than being unable to recall vital data. Suppose one is stopped for a minor traffic violation and is unable to give the inquiring officer the correct name, birth date, etc. It is a known fact that Government clerks often try to catch illegal passport applicants by inquiring into detailed personal data about the applicant.

The New State ID Card

The next sequential step in preparing for a complete fade is the acquisition of an official State-issued ID card. One should not be tempted to bypass this step and skip ahead to the premature acquisition of a new drivers license. Most States are much less critical on the requirements for an ID card than they are a drivers license. The purpose is to obtain that necessary "second ID" that will provide the requirements for obtaining a new drivers license! Armed with a newly acquired birth certificate this becomes a simple matter. As in all other aspects of executing a successful fade, be prepared in advance. Call ahead to check on individual requirements.

Most States issue their ID cards at the Department of Motor Vehicles. Often this will be the same department where drivers licenses are processed. Check the appendices for additional information.

Some States require two forms of ID for verification prior to issuing a State ID card. If two forms of ID are required, the documention is usually easy to generate or alter (such as W2 forms, church records, medical records, immunization records; even prescriptions are often acceptable). A church blessing certificate is usually acceptable if a birth certificate is not available.

Be aware that some Government Agencies will not mail official documentation to a post office box. This minor problem is easily overcome by selecting a mail drop that offers the use of a street address (see establishing a mail drop located elsewhere in this book). Some States request fingerprints for drivers licenses and State ID cards. For obvious reasons, this request is always declined.

Now is the time to allow the newly acquired documents to "season a bit." Both the birth certificate and the ID card will likely show recent issue dates. Don't rush things by applying for additional documents too soon. An attentive clerk might become suspicious if he/she sees too many documents being issued within a short timeframe. Highway Patrol officers are also very adept at spotting close issue dates on identification documents.

The New Drivers License

When applying for a new drivers license, several precautions should be observed. For obvious reasons, the address used on the application should be that of a mail drop. In fact, it is considered wise to generate a mail drop for the sole purpose of receiving a drivers license.

Upon receipt of the license, the mail drop is discontinued, never to be used again.

This move virtually erases any traceable connection between the address of the recipient and the Department of Motor Vehicles.

Because of the crackdown on convicted drivers involved in "driving under the influence" (DUI), many are attempting to obtain original licenses by fraudulent means. This could prompt a thorough check of support ID. However, with the documentation already obtained, coupled with proper planning and carefuly study of the documents, few problems should be encountered.

When applying for an original drivers license, an old one will not be available to surrender. This may provoke added suspicion if the applicant is over twenty-one. If questioned as to the reason, do not panic. There are many perfectly valid explanations for not possessing a drivers license, even for the middle-aged. For example, living outside the country for a number of years, or residing in large, congested, Eastern cities. New York City, especially Manhattan, has thousands of adult residents who do not own a drivers license. Many have never driven! Often owning a car in large cities can be a financial burden as well as an inconvenience because of parking, having to lease a garage (sometimes a long way from where one lives), and the convenience of public transportation. Serving overseas in the military, religious missions, medical problems, etc., are all valid reasons for mature males not owning a drivers license. Most drivers license agencies encounter similar situations regularly.

When applying for an original drivers license, a drivers test will be required. This will necessitate the use of an automobile for the driving portion of the test. If one's personal vehicle is used (as is usually the case), the examiner may ask to see the registration. This situation almost always causes panic on the applicant's part when questioned about the name of the owner of the vehicle as it appears on the registration. Have a convincing story prepared in advance, and don't be caught off guard.

After receiving the new drivers' license, it is a simple matter to transfer a registration (depending on individual State law) from one name to another.

If the stratagies as outlined have been followed, one should have in his possession three State-issued forms of identification: a certified birth certificate, ID card, and drivers license. With these documents, the persecuted male is coming ever closer to becoming a new and transparent identity among the masses. The old self will become more obsolete and invisible with the passing of each day. To those who search, the trail becomes fainter and fainter, and frustration mounts because the opportunity to humiliate and degrade a once-proud male is slipping quietly away.

Supporting ID

Now is the proper time to gather the rest of also very important support documentation by using your newly acquired ID. A collection of additional items will solidify and reinforce the new documents you've so painstakingly obtained.

Excellent supporting ID could consist of:

1. Banking records: deposits, withdrawal slips, statements, automatic teller cards, etc.
2. Library card
3. Prescriptions
4. Immunization records (very valuable!)
5. Medical records
6. Church documents (membership, baptism, blessing, etc.)
7. Insurance policies
8. Voter registration
9. Fraternal organization ID

The above list is only a small fraction of easily obtainable support documents. Of the list, two of the items are to be considered as exceptional and should be considered welcome additions to any complete fade portfolio.

UNITED STATES DEPARTMENT OF STATE

APPLICATION FOR PASSPORT REGISTRATION

SEE INSTRUCTIONS—TYPE OR PRINT IN INK IN WHITE AREAS

1. NAME FIRST NAME | MIDDLE NAME

LAST NAME

2. MAILING ADDRESS

STREET

CITY, STATE, ZIP CODE

COUNTRY | IN CARE OF

☐ 5 Yr. ☐ 10 Yr. | Issue Date ______

R D O DP

End. #______ | Exp. ______

3. SEX Male Female | 4. PLACE OF BIRTH City, State or Province, Country | 5. DATE OF BIRTH Mo. Day Year | 6. SEE FEDERAL TAX LAW NOTICE ON REVERSE SIDE | SOCIAL SECURITY NUMBER

7. HEIGHT Feet Inches | 8. COLOR OF HAIR | 9. COLOR OF EYES | 10. (Area Code) HOME PHONE | 11. (Area Code) BUSINESS PHONE

12. PERMANENT ADDRESS (Street, City, State, ZIP Code) | 13. OCCUPATION

FOLD

14. FATHER'S NAME | BIRTHPLACE | BIRTH DATE | U.S. CITIZEN ☐ YES ☐ NO

15. MOTHER'S MAIDEN NAME | BIRTHPLACE | BIRTH DATE | U.S. CITIZEN ☐ YES ☐ NO

16. TRAVEL PLANS *(Not Mandatory)* COUNTRIES | DEPARTURE DATE | LENGTH OF STAY

17. HAVE YOU EVER BEEN ISSUED A U.S. PASSPORT? YES ☐ NO ☐ IF YES, SUBMIT PASSPORT IF AVAILABLE. ☐ Submitted

IF UNABLE TO SUBMIT MOST RECENT PASSPORT, STATE ITS DISPOSITION: COMPLETE NEXT LINE

NAME IN WHICH ISSUED | PASSPORT NUMBER | ISSUE DATE (Mo., Day, Yr.) | DISPOSITION

SUBMIT TWO RECENT IDENTICAL PHOTOS

2" × 2"

FROM 1" TO 1-3/8"

18. HAVE YOU EVER BEEN MARRIED? ☐ YES ☐ NO | DATE OF MOST RECENT MARRIAGE Mo. Day Year

WIDOWED/DIVORCED? ☐ YES ☐ NO | IF YES, GIVE DATE Mo. Day Year

SPOUSE'S FULL BIRTH NAME | SPOUSE'S BIRTHPLACE

19. IN CASE OF EMERGENCY, NOTIFY *(Person Not Traveling With You)* *(Not Mandatory)* | RELATIONSHIP

FULL NAME

ADDRESS | (Area Code) PHONE NUMBER

20. TO BE COMPLETED BY AN APPLICANT WHO BECAME A CITIZEN THROUGH NATURALIZATION

I IMMIGRATED TO THE U.S. (Month, Year) | I RESIDED CONTINUOUSLY IN THE U.S. From (Mo., Yr.) To (Mo., Yr.) | DATE NATURALIZED (Mo., Day, Yr.) | PLACE

FOLD

21. DO NOT SIGN APPLICATION UNTIL REQUESTED TO DO SO BY PERSON ADMINISTERING OATH

I have not, since acquiring United States citizenship, performed any of the acts listed under "Acts or Conditions" on the reverse of this application form (unless explanatory statement is attached). I solemnly swear (or affirm) that the statements made on this application are true and the photograph attached is a true likeness of me.

Subscribed and sworn to (affirmed) before me

Month Day Year | (SEAL) | X

☒ Clerk of Court or ☐ PASSPORT Agent

☐ Postal Employee

☐ (Vice) Consul USA At ______

(Signature of person authorized to accept application) | *(Sign in presence of person authorized to accept application)*

22. APPLICANT'S IDENTIFYING DOCUMENTS ☐ PASSPORT ☐ DRIVER'S LICENSE ☐ OTHER (Specify) | No.

ISSUE DATE Month Day Year | EXPIRATION DATE Month Day Year | PLACE OF ISSUE | ISSUED IN THE NAME OF

23. FOR ISSUING OFFICE USE ONLY (Applicant's evidence of citizenship)

☐ Birth Cert. SR CR City Filed/Issued:

☐ Passport Bearer's Name:

☐ Report of Birth

☐ Naturalization/Citizenship Cert. No.:

☐ Other:

☐ Seen & Returned

☐ Attached

APPLICATION APPROVAL

Examiner Name

Office, Date

24. FEE ______ EXEC. ______ POST ______

PAGE 75A

FORM DSP-11 (12-87) | (SEE INSTRUCTIONS ON REVERSE) | Form Approved OMB No. 1405-0004 (Exp. 8/1/89)

UNITED STATES DEPARTMENT OF STATE

PASSPORT APPLICATION

FEDERAL TAX LAW:

Section 6039E of the Internal Revenue Code of 1986 requires a passport applicant to provide his/her name (#1), mailing address (#2), date of birth (#5), and social security number (#6). If you have not been issued a social security number, enter zeroes in box #6. Passport Services will provide this information to the Internal Revenue Service routinely. Any applicant who fails to provide the required information is subject to a $500 penalty enforced by the IRS. All questions on this matter should be referred to the nearest IRS office.

ACTS OR CONDITIONS

(If any of the below-mentioned acts or conditions has been performed by or applies to the applicant, the portion which applies should be lined out, and a supplementary explanatory statement under oath (or affirmation) by the applicant should be attached and made a part of this application.)

I have not, since acquiring United States citizenship, been naturalized as a citizen of a foreign state; taken an oath or made an affirmation or other formal declaration of allegiance to a foreign state; entered or served in the armed forces of a foreign state; accepted or performed the duties of any office, post, or employment under the government of a foreign state or political subdivision thereof; made a formal renunciation of nationality either in the United States or before a diplomatic or consular officer of the United States in a foreign state; or been convicted by a court or court martial of competent jurisdiction of committing any act of treason against, or attempting by force to overthrow, or bearing arms against, the United States, or conspiring to overthrow, put down, or to destroy by force, the Government of the United States; or having been naturalized, within one year after such naturalization, returned to the country of my birth or any other foreign country to take up a permanent residence.

WARNING: False statements made knowingly and willfully in passport applications or in affidavits or other supporting documents submitted therewith are punishable by fine and/or imprisonment under provisions of 18 USC 1001 and/or 18 USC 1542. Alteration or mutilation of a passport issued pursuant to this application is punishable by fine and/or imprisonment under the provisions of 18 USC 1543. The use of a passport in violation of the restrictions contained therein or of the passport regulations is punishable by fine and/or imprisonment under 18 USC 1544. All statements and documents submitted are subject to verification.

PRIVACY ACT STATEMENT:

The information solicited on this form is authorized by, but not limited to, those statutes codified in Titles 8, 18, and 22, United States Code, and all predecessor statutes whether or not codified, and all regulations issued pursuant to Executive Order 11295 of August 5, 1966. The primary purpose for soliciting the information is to establish citizenship, identity, and entitlement to issuance of a United States Passport or related facility, and to properly administer and enforce the laws pertaining thereto.

The information is made available as a routine use on a need-to-know basis to personnel of the Department of State and other government agencies having statutory or other lawful authority to maintain such information in the performance of their official duties; pursuant to a court order; and, as set forth in Part 171, Title 22, Code of Federal Regulations (see *Federal Register,* Volume 42, pages 49791 through 49795).

Failure to provide the information requested on this form may result in the denial of a United States Passport, related document, or service to the individual seeking such passport, document, or service.

HOW TO APPLY FOR A U.S. PASSPORT. U.S. passports are issued only to U.S. citizens or nationals. Each person must obtain his or her own passport.

IF YOU ARE A FIRST-TIME APPLICANT, please complete and submit this application in person. (Applicants under 13 years of age usually need not appear in person unless requested. A parent or guardian may execute the application on the child's behalf.) Each application must be accompanied by (1) PROOF OF U.S. CITIZENSHIP, (2) PROOF OF IDENTITY, (3) TWO PHOTOGRAPHS, (4) FEES (as explained below) to one of the following acceptance agents: a clerk of any Federal or State court of record or a judge or clerk of any probate court accepting applications; a designated postal employee at a selected post office; or an agent at a Passport Agency in Boston, Chicago, Honolulu, Houston, Los Angeles, Miami, New Orleans, New York, Philadelphia, San Francisco, Seattle, Stamford, or Washington, D.C.; or a U.S. consular official.

IF YOU HAVE HAD A PREVIOUS PASSPORT, inquire about eligibility to use Form DSP-82 (mail-in application).

Address requests for passport amendment, extension of validity, or additional visa pages to a Passport Agency or a U.S. Consulate or Embassy abroad. Check visa requirements with consular officials of countries to be visited well in advance of your departure.

(1) PROOF OF U.S. CITIZENSHIP.

(a) APPLICANTS BORN IN THE UNITED STATES. Submit previous U.S. passport or **certified** birth certificate. A birth certificate must include your given name and surname, date and place of birth, date the birth record was filed, and seal or other certification of the official custodian of such records. A record filed more than 1 year after the birth is acceptable if it is supported by evidence described in the next paragraph.

IF NO BIRTH RECORD EXISTS, submit registrar's notice to that effect. Also submit an early baptismal or circumcision certificate, hospital birth record, early census, school, or family Bible records, newspaper or insurance files, or notarized affidavits of persons having knowledge of your birth (preferably with at least one record listed above). Evidence should include your given name and surname, date and place of birth, and seal or other certification of office (if customary) and signature of issuing official.

(b) APPLICANTS BORN OUTSIDE THE UNITED STATES. Submit previous U.S. passport or Certificate of Naturalization, or Certificate of Citizenship, or a Report of Birth Abroad, or evidence described below.

IF YOU CLAIM CITIZENSHIP THROUGH NATURALIZATION OF PARENT(S), submit the Certificate(s) of Naturalization of your parent(s), your foreign birth certificate, and proof of your admission to the United States for permanent residence.

IF YOU CLAIM CITIZENSHIP THROUGH BIRTH ABROAD TO U.S. CITIZEN PARENT(S), submit a Consular Report of Birth (Form FS-240) or Certification of Birth (Form DS-1350 or FS-545), or your foreign birth certificate, parents' marriage certificate, proof of citizenship of your parent(s), and affidavit of U.S. citizen parent(s) showing all periods and places of residence/physical presence in the United States and abroad before your birth.

(2) PROOF OF IDENTITY. If you are not personally known to the acceptance agent, you must establish your identity to the agent's satisfaction. You may submit items such as the following containing your signature AND physical description or photograph that is a good likeness of you: previous U.S. passport; Certificate of Naturalization or of Citizenship; driver's license (not temporary or learner's license); or government (Federal, State, municipal) identification card or pass. Temporary or altered documents are not acceptable.

IF YOU CANNOT PROVE YOUR IDENTITY as stated above, you must appear with an IDENTIFYING WITNESS who is a U.S. citizen or permanent resident alien who has known you for at least 2 years. Your witness must prove his or her identity and complete and sign an Affidavit of Identifying Witness (Form DSP-71) before the acceptance agent. You must also submit some identification of your own.

(3) TWO PHOTOGRAPHS. Submit two identical photographs of you alone, sufficiently recent to be a good likeness (normally taken within the last 6 months), 2 × 2 inches in size, with an image size from bottom of chin to top of head (including hair) of between 1 and 1-3/8 inches. Photographs must be clear, front view, full face, taken in normal street attire without a hat or dark glasses, and printed on thin paper with a plain light (white or off-white) background. They may be black and white or color. They must be capable of withstanding a mounting temperature of 225° Fahrenheit (107° Celsius). Photographs retouched so that your appearance is changed are unacceptable. Snapshots, most vending machine prints, and magazine or full-length photographs are unacceptable.

(4) FEES. Submit $42 if you are 18 years of age or older. The passport fee is $35. In addition, a fee of $7 is charged for the execution of the application. Your passport will be valid for 10 years from the date of issue except where limited by the Secretary of State to a shorter period. Submit $27 if you are under 18 years of age. The passport fee is $20 and the execution fee is $7. Your passport will be valid for 5 years from the date of issue, except where limited as above.

Pay the passport and execution fees in one of the following forms: checks—personal, certified, traveler's; bank draft or cashier's check; money order, U.S. Postal, international, currency exchange; or if abroad, the foreign currency equivalent, or a check drawn on a U.S. bank.

Make passport and execution fees payable to Passport Services (except if applying at a State court, pay execution fee as the State court requires) or the appropriate Embassy or Consulate, if abroad. No fee is charged to applicants with U.S. Government or military authorization for no-fee passports (except State courts may collect the execution fee). Pay special postage if applicable.

FORM DSP 11
12-87

The first is the immunization booklet/record as provided by the U.S. Department of Health, Education, and Welfare. These are the vaccination records provided for world travelers, generally combined with passports. This document is acceptable ID by the Social Security office when applying for a new card.

This immunization record is also approved by the "World Health Organization." The form is available from many private physicians. If in doubt as to where to obtain such service, simply call the US Postal Service (passport information) nearest you, and inquire what physicians in the area provide such services. One may suffer a small amount of discomfort from the vaccinations, but the inconvenience is well worth obtaining that documentation. Any standard immunization record, be it Federal, State, or private, can be considered a valuable enhancement to the "complete fade" portfolio.

Church documentation lends a great deal of credibility to any fading effort. Even if some small amount of time must be spent attending a few services, it is well worth it.

It should be noted that church baptismal records are often accepted at face value in the place of a birth certificate by the Social Security office or other Federal and State organizations. Researching newspaper microfilm libraries for burned or other-wise destroyed churches whose records were lost, is an excellent way for creating church documentation. The possibilities are endless!

The New Social Security Card

Obtaining a new Social Security card would be the next logical step on the way to your complete fade. The best, and by far the most convenient method is if a namesake had a Social Security card issued before his death. Then simply apply for a duplicate card! The documents already gathered should be more that sufficient for this purpose. The value of this procedure would depend entirely on the Social Security office having never been informed of the card owner's death! This must be checked out by checking with the Social Security office for verification. Valid reasons are necessary before the Social Security office will give out this type of information, but a little homework and originality should produce the desired results. (EDITORS NOTE: to list, or give examples of acceptable reasons would only serve to destroy their usefulness! This volume will be studied by the proper authorities in order to close the still existing loopholes!).

The second method is to make use of the resources in the portfolio, and apply for a new Social Security card. As previously mentioned, an adult male applying for a new card would almost certainly be thoroughly scrutinized as being suspect. Many persecuted males claim they have successfully overcome these barriers with the proper preparation and have successfully been issued new cards.

The most formidable barrier to overcome would be why, as a mature adult, a Social Security card had never previously been issued? Social Security personnel would have to be thoroughly convinced that there was never any reportable income earned in the USA!

However, it is the law and duty of the Social Security office to issue a card to every wage earner. Without a Social Security, Uncle Sam cannot collect Social Security installments!

Recently enacted legislation now specifies that all children five years and over who are listed as dependants on the 1987 and later tax returns must have a Social Security card. It is apparent that "Big Brother" is slowly but very systematically removing many of our freedoms as a means of Government convenience, and especially, Government control. The day of the "national ID card" is very near! At that time, one may be required to show a numbered ID card to any requesting officer of the law. It has been reported that a past, well-known female member of Congress once sponsored a bill to have all new-born infants identified with a number tatooed on the sole of the right foot!

This is very reminiscent of the marking of the Jews by the Germans during the years of the Holocaust!

The new Social Security requirments recently passed by Congress have themselves generated the third method. The Social Security office is working overtime, even on Saturdays, to keep up with these new demands. To apply for a Social Security card, two items are required. First, a certified copy of a birth certificate or church blessing certificate, and Second, one form of recent ID for each child. "Recent ID" means any record not more than one year old, such as immunization records, medical records or cards, prescriptions, school or church records, etc. <u>Applicants under 18 need not be present</u>.

What this means to those embarking on a complete fade is an opportunity to obtain an unshared Social Security number. By generating and obtaining the necessary documents, one can obtain a new Social Security card using the adopted name. This is usually accopmlished by generating an unverifiable church blessing certificate (from burned or destroyed religious institutions), to create an applicant under five years of age with no school history. Granted, the birth date as it appears in the Social Security department files will be in error with that of the actual card holder, but this in itself should cause few, if any, problems. It could always be explained as a typographical error, especially if the dates used were very similar to the namesake's, maybe slightly transposed. Because of age variances, this number <u>is not</u> used on passport applications. Some persecuted males have reportedly enlisted the assistance of women accomplices to portray the applicant's mother.

Obtaining A Passport

A United States passport is the ultimate in personal ID documents. Unless international travel is planned, the acquisition of a passort for ID purposes is not necessary. In fact, it could be considered as overkill. To show a passport in response to an ordinary ID request, (cashing checks, opening bank accounts etc.) would likely cause undue suspicion. However, if visiting other countries is anticipated, a passport is an absolute necessity.

At the present time, there are an estimated thirteen million U.S. passports in circulation. U.S. passports are distributed from the General Passport office in Washington, D.C. Application can be made throughout the fifty States at designated passport agencies. Call the local Post Office for information on applying for a passport in the area of choice. The passport office requires a personal appearance to file an application. A passport application form can be found later in this chapter. The passport office requires two recent photographs along with acceptable identification, and a $35.00 filing fee, plus a $7.00 executing fee.

The <u>only</u> <u>acceptable</u> proof of US citizenship required for a passport is an <u>official</u> <u>State</u>-issued birth certificate, <u>certified</u> with a registrar's signature and the raised, impressed, <u>or multi</u>colored seal of the office. Secondary documents to prove citizenship include a baptismal certificate, certificate of circumcision, hospital birth record, early census, school, or family bible records are no longer accepted as they were in the past. In addition to proof of US citizenship, a document of identification such as a Drivers' License, State or Federal ID cards, or Government pass is acceptable.

Be aware that obtaining a US passport with borrowed documents will require the utmost in homework and planning! Government personnel who issue and process US passports are trained and skilled in detecting fraud. Do not underestimate their knowledge and/or talents. It is always best to apply for a passport at the smaller, rural areas of the US. Avoid the larger coastal cities such as Los Angeles, San Francisco, New York, etc.. Cities on the Mexican and Canadian border are also off limits for the cautious passport applicant.

When applying for a passport, the procedure is similar to this: the documents and application will be examined completely by the passport agent. The applicant will be carefully watched for any outward signs of nervousness. The agent may ask some pointed "off the wall" questions in an attempt to force errors or nervousness. Most of the questions will be centered around the information provided on the application. He/she might say to the applicant: "I see that your father has passed away, where was he buried?" Or, "your application shows you were born in Canton, Ohio. Did you attend school there? What high school?" As can be seen, the applicant must be prepared or he might face detection!

If the agent is satisfied with the short interview, a passport will be issued in approximately five weeks. Verification of the birth record and Social Security number should be complete at the end of this time. If the agent feels something is wrong, and the applicant fits the proper "profile of suspicion," a complete verification procedure will take place. All of the data provided will be checked out, as well as the individual.

Men entering a complete fade generally have accumulated the necessary authentic documents which will stand up under investigation. However, they must also school themselves and be thoroughly familiar with the facts, names, dates, and places associated with the new identity. It would, however, be an error in judgement to memorize too many insignificant details about the new ID. This in itself might cause suspicion!

If the basics are memorized, saying, "I don't know" to a question that normally would not be generally known, is perfectly acceptable. As an example, if the agent asked the applicant: "Where were your mother and father married?", very few applicants would be able to provide this type of information. If immediate answers to this type of questions were provided, it could very well cause undue suspicion.

When the passport is issued, one of the photographs supplied will be glued firmly to one of the pages in the front of the passport. The second photograph will remain with the application and be retained in the US State Department files. The applicant will be required to sign the passport in two different places. One of the signatures will be on the left margin of the attached photo, the other will be on the physical description page as the signature of the bearer.

The passport agent will then use two seals to validate the passport. The first will imprint the Seal of the USA, an eagle with an outer ring which says: "United States of America, Department of State", in the center of the glued-on photograph. The second Seal is usually square in nature and is imprinted on the right margin of the photo. These embossing Seals provide a colored (usually red and blue) imprint that indicates: "Photo Attached, Department of State," and the name of the city in which the passport was issued, New York, San Francisco, etc.

Establishing Credit

It is assumed that one now possesses a complete portfolio on the chosen namesake. If the added risks of a credit investigation are accepted, building a totally new and untarnished credit rating becomes a simple matter. Nevertheless, anyone who avails himself of established credit procedures will automatically invoke a loss of personal privacy. The best known method to establish a new credit rating is by obtaining a nationally recognized credit card such as Mastercard or Visa, and then slowly build a credit history by judicial use of the cards. Obtaining a credit card with no prior credit history simply requires an interest-bearing investment, generally from $300.00 to a $1,000.00.

On occasions, some banks will assist new depositors in establishing credit and issue a credit card with a much lower specified balance. There are any number of banks and financial institutions willing to issue a Mastercard and/or Visa to an individual with no prior credit history, even bad credit! The main requirement is that a savings account be established at their institution and the maintaining of a specified minimum balance.

The line of credit offered is usually from 50% to 80% of the specified minimum balance. This arrangement is usually referred to as a "Secured Credit Card Account." This type of savings account will pay interest and the time requirement is generally for no longer than a year. If, after a year, a satisfactory payment history has been established and maintained, the minimum balance requirement is withdrawn, and the credit rating established.

Banks and other lending institutions are always looking for depositors. Either call or visit any bank or savings and loan company, and inquire about a minimum balance, secured credit card account.

If difficulities are experienced in locating an agreeable financial institution, try any of the following:

Key Federal Savings Bank
626 Revolution Street
Havre de Grace, Md. 21078

(A minimum of $500.00 is required.)

American National Bank of New York
Box C, Fleischmanns
New York, N.Y. 12430
Minimum deposit $1,000.00 plus $35.00 annual fee

State Street Bank and Trust of Boston
225 Franklin Street
Boston, Mass 02110

$5,000.00 deposit plus a $50.00 annual fee

Timesaver Inc.
12276 Wilkins Ave.
Rockville, Md. 20852

Bell Savings and Loan Association
279 Arlington Ave, Kensington, Ca. 94707

Household Federal Savings
P.O. Box 20919, El.Cajon, CA 92021

Franklin Savings and Loan
1201 Market St. at Eigth, San Francisco, Ca. 94103

For a more complete listing of institutions interested in establishing secured credit card accounts consult the classified sections in the national news magazines, such as National Inquirer, Star, Globe, etc. The adds usually claim credit cards issued regardless of credit history. Be aware that the services being offered in these adds are no more than the information shown in these few paragraphs. In addition, a healthy charge is usually assessed.

Keeping A Low Profile

"In a sense, a person is defined by the checks he writes. By examining them, the agent gets to know his doctors, lawyers, creditors, political allies, social connections, religious affiliations, educational interests, the papers and magazines he reads and so on ad infinitum."

Justice William O. Douglas

Those who achieve the highest level of privacy in America today are the very rich, the very poor, and the criminal element. If wealthy enough, one can be exempt from many of the investigations most other citizens are routinely subjected to. There would be no need to establish credit. All bills and expenses could be paid by cash or money order, leaving few, if any, traceable paper tracks. Many very rich Americans have most of their cash assets deposited in offshore banks to eliminate unwanted intrusions and risks by State and Federal Agencies. A person's personal finances can be kept a secret, and this translates to personal privacy.

The very poor have also achieved a high degree of personal privacy, not because of a deliberate and conscious effort on their own, but simply because no one cares. These are the street people, illegal aliens, migrant workers, and those who have lost interest in life itself. These poor souls have been excused from accountability by a non-caring society because of their lack of economic standing in the community. These people have, in their own way, eliminated themselves from filing forms, paying taxes, or even being counted in a census report.

Professional criminals must acheive a very high degree of privacy as a matter of survival. These people leave few, if any, paper tracks behind which could be used as incriminating evidence. Practically all transactions are handled with cash. They have no credit cards, and fill out no personal documents. Assets are either deposited offshore or very carefully hidden. Most of their homes and vehicles are leased or rented. Phone calls are made from pay telephones. The professional has learned to protect his privacy by protecting his assets.

The common denominator involved in all three of the preceding examples on maintaining privacy, is money. How one uses and dispenses liquid assets can be a major threat to the privacy, or, as the case is here, the freedom of the man living in the shadows. Any time he opens a checking or savings account or applies for credit, he is opening the door to invasion into his privacy, and if carelessly done, he endangers his freedom.

Achieving and maintaining a low profile is mostly common sense. By far the biggest threat to any man living in the shadows is exposure by an informer. As mentioned previously, that danger cannot be overemphasized.

After successfully entering a complete fade, the persecuted male will want to enjoy his newfound freedom. If he is judicial in his financial transactions and does not divulge any personal information to others, freedom is for the taking. May all men living in the shadows enjoy and relish this new adventure.

As an ancient philosopher once said, "May the wind always be at your back."

APPENDIX 1

SOCIAL SECURITY CARDS

The Social Security Act in the United States had its begining under then President Franklin D. Roosevelt in 1935. The program had the wellfare of the wage earner in mind by providing protection against financial disaster. The original program provided insurance for old age, survivors, and disability. From its inception until 1974, Social Security cards were issued in the name of an individual by simply submitting an application. No ID or verification was required.

After 1974 the Department of Social Security started to change its application requirements because of abuses, mostly from individuals fraudulently claiming benefits under more than one number. Some Federal and State Agencies also started to abuse the intended purpose of the Social Security number because of its inherent uniqueness. Because present laws require practically all Americans to have a Social Security number, we have, in effect become serialized. The Social Security number has become the accepted means of personal identification, similar to the methods used by corrections institutions when assigning numbers to prison inmates. Politicians often boast on how they have voted against any bills requiring Americans to carry a Federal ID card, but the abusive use of the Social Security cards has produced the same result.

The Government has now begun to issue new Social Security cards made of counterfeit-resistant stock. The new red, white and blue cards are already in use. If one should apply for a replacement, the new type will replace the old thin cardboard-style card used for so many years. The new cards are printed on the same type of durable bank-note paper used in printing most of the world's currencies. Officials of the Bureau of Printing and Engraving, and the Secret Service say it is the most counterfeit-resistant paper available anywhere. The old style cardboard cards issued over the last 48 years <u>are still valid</u> and replacement is <u>not</u> required.

The new counterfeit-resistant cards are required under the Social Security bail-out law passed by Congress and signed by then President Reagan. The purpose of the new law is to reduce the fifteen billion dollar-a-year losses blamed on crimes involving people who use false identification, which of course includes false Social Security numbers.

Social Security Administration spokesman James Brown said "The new cards by themselves cannot stop these crimes. It'll do some good in the sense that it will be difficult (for counterfeiters) to make this card, and difficult to alter it, but many problems will continue since birth certificates and other documents needed to obtain Social Security cards can still be counterfeited, and since millions of Americans will continue to carry the old cards."

A new law has recently been passed by Congress which requires all Americans to file for a "work permit" and verify citizenship at the same time in order to be legally employed. The burden would fall on the employer to verify documentation. Theoretically, a hot line would be set up to verify Social Security numbers, names, etc.

This is another prime example of the bureaucratic lunacy so rampant in some of our elected representatives. There always exists, within those in power, the willingness to destroy the freedoms and liberty of the multitudes in order to solve a minorities' problem.

Eventually, all Americans will fall victim to Federal Form I-9, which is a feature of the Immigration Reform and Control Act known as the "Employment Eligibility Verification Program."

To apply for a Social Security card, two documents must be provided: the first is "evidence of age and citizenship," and the second is "evidence of identity." The following documents are acceptable proof of age and citizenship: birth certificate, church record of birth, or blessing certificate.

If these are not available, the following are acceptable substitutes: school records, immunization records, mecical records or cards, prescriptions, church records, State or Federal census records, insurance policies, marriage records, military discharge papers, delayed birth certificate, draft card, or any other record, which shows age or date of birth. Evidence of identity might be documents such as a drivers' license, state ID card, voter registration card, school identification card, work badge or building pass, draft card or military ID, US passport, US ID card, credit card with signature, library card with signature, plus any other documents which show either an individual's signature or photograph.

In generating Social Security numbers a particuliar code is used. The first group of three digits is assigned to a particular State. The second set of two digits, (in coded form), represent either the year of birth, or the year of application. The last four digits are called the "citizen's numbers". There are no Social Security numbers begining with "8" or "9". As of now, these particular digits have not yet been assigned and are therefore not used.

The following is a State-by-State listing of the first three digits assigned to them by the Department of Social Security.

Alabama	416-424	Montana	516-517
Alaska	574	Nebraska	505-508
Arizona	526-527	Nevada	530
Arkansas	429-432	New Hampshire	001-003
California	545-573	New Jersey	135-158
Colorado	521-524	New Mexico	525-585
Connecticut	040-049	New York	050-134
Delaware	221-222	North Carolina	237-246
D.C.	577-579	North Dakota	501-502
Florida	261-267	Ohio	268-302
Georgia	252-260	Oklahoma	440-448
Hawaii	575-576	Oregon	540-544
Idaho	518-519	Pennsylvania	159-211
Illinois	318-361	Rhode Island	035-039
Indiana	303-317	South Carolina	247-251
Iowa	478-485	South Dakota	503-504
Kansas	509-515	Tennessee	408-415
Kentucky	400-407	Texas	449-467
Louisiana	433-439	Utah	528-529
Maine	004-007	Vermont	008-009
Maryland	212-220	Virginia	223-231
Massachusetts	010-034	Washington	531-539
Michigan	362-386	West Virginia	223-231
Minnesota	468-386	Wisconsin	387-399
Mississippi	425-428	Wyoming	520
Missouri	486-500		

Additions

Arizona	600-601	Mississippi	587-588
California	602-626	New Mexico	585
Florida	589-595	North Carolina	232

Miscellaneous

Virgin Islands	580
Puerto Rico	580-584
Guam, Samoa & Pacific Terr.	586
Railroad Ret.	700-728

HOW TO APPLY FOR AN ORIGINAL OR REPLACEMENT SOCIAL SECURITY NUMBER CARD

Before completing this application, read the information below, the completion instructions on page 2 and the Privacy Act information on page 4. The Social Security Administration does not charge a fee for Social Security cards and there is no need to pay anyone for this service.

WHERE TO APPLY

Mail or take your evidence documents and application to the nearest Social Security office. However, you must apply in person at a Social Security office if:

1. You are age 18 or older and have never had a Social Security number card before, or
2. You are an alien whose immigration documents should not be mailed.

EVIDENCE YOU WILL NEED

Social Security law requires that you furnish evidence of your age, identity, and U.S. citizenship or lawful alien status. Find one of the four categories below which applies to you and read the instructions carefully. If you apply for a Social Security number for your child or other individual for whom you are legal guardian or legal custodian, you must also furnish evidence of your identity (see list B Below).

You must submit original or certified documents as evidence — we cannot accept uncertified or notarized photocopies. We will return all documents submitted. NOTE: all documents submitted as evidence may be retained temporarily and verified with the custodian of the original records.

If you have any questions or need help in obtaining your documents, please call or visit your nearest Social Security office.

1. U.S. Citizen — Born in the U.S. — Applying for original Social Security number

Please submit one document from list A. **and** at least one from list B.

List A. Evidence of Age and Citizenship
One of the following records established before your 5th birthday:

- Public birth certificate (**This is the preferred document.** You should submit it if at all possible.)
- Religious record showing age or date of birth (To establish citizenship, it must have been recorded within 3 months of birth.)
- Hospital record of birth

If your birth was never recorded or the public record no longer exists, submit documents from list B for evidence of age and citizenship. At least one document must show your name, age or date of birth, and your place of birth. It should be at least one year old.

List B. Evidence of Identity
A public or hospital birth record is not considered evidence of identity. An identity document should contain enough information to identify you. Some items we look for on the document are name, age, address, signature, physical description and picture. Examples are:

- Identity card
- Driver's license
- Adoption record
- Insurance policy
- Youth organization record
- School record
- Medical record
- Work badge or building pass
- Military record
- Court order for name change
- Marriage or Divorce record
- U.S. Passport
- U.S. Citizen ID card
- Religious record (If not submitted as evidence of age)
- Any other document providing identifying data sufficient to establish proper identity.

2. U.S. Citizen — Born outside the U.S.—Applying for Original Social Security Number

If you were born outside the U.S. but are a U.S. citizen you should submit either:

a. U.S. consular report of birth (FS-240 or FS-545) **and** evidence of your identity (see category 1, list B);

OR

b. Your foreign birth certificate (if not readily available, another document showing age or date of birth) **and** one of the following:

- U.S. citizen ID card
- Citizenship certificate
- U.S. passport
- Certificate of Naturalization

3. Alien — Not a U.S. Citizen Applying for Original Social Security Number

If you are an alien living in or visiting the U.S., you should bring in your foreign birth certificate (if available) or passport **and** one or more of the folllowing:

- Alien Registration Receipt Card I-151 or I-551.
- U.S. Immigration Form I-94 (and I-20ID, if applicable), I-181a, I-185, I-186, I-210, or I-586 (and I-444, if applicable)

NOTE: If you are a lawfully admitted alien *but not permitted to work* and you have a valid non- work need for a Social Security number, we will issue you a number if you present evidence of such need. However, the card will show that the number is not valid for employment. If you ever use the number in a job, we will notify INS. In addition, any information obtained in connection with this application can be given to INS.

4. Any Applicant Requesting a Replacement Card (Duplicate or Correction)

You must present at least evidence of your identity such as one or more of the documents in categories 1 (List B), 2 or 3. In addition, if you are foreign-born (or U.S.-born but no longer a U.S. citizen), you must submit evidence of your current U.S. citizenship or lawful alien status. After we examine your documents, you may be asked for additional evidence of your age, or U.S. citizenship or lawful alien status.

If you are changing your name, you must provide evidence identifying you under both your **old** and **new** names. We will accept one document if it shows both the old and new names or multiple documents if each shows only one name. If the name change is due to marriage or divorce, your marriage certificate or divorce decree is usually sufficient if it shows both your previous and new names.

Form SS-5 (11-86)
5/84, 1/85 and 8/85 editions may be used until supply is exhausted

IMPORTANT REMINDERS

EVIDENCE

An applicant for a Social Security number card must provide evidence of age, identity, and U.S. citizenship or lawful alien status. See page 1 of the application to see what evidence is needed.

All documents submitted as evidence must be either the originals or copies certified by the issuing agency. We do not accept uncertified or notarized copies.

PERSONAL INTERVIEW

An applicant must apply in person if he/she is age 18 or older and has never had a Social Security number card before.

COMPLETING THE APPLICATION

Type or print your answers on the application. **Use dark blue or black ink.** If you do not know and cannot find the answer to a question, enter the word "unknown" in the space for the answer.

INSTRUCTIONS FOR COMPLETING SOME QUESTIONS ON THE APPLICATION FORM

The instructions below are numbered to correspond with the numbered items on the application.

1. Enter your full name as you use it for work, school, or other official business. If you have a middle name, enter it in full in the space provided. Only your first name, middle initial and last name will appear on the card itself, unless you specifically request that we spell out your middle name.

   If your name has changed, show the name you were given at birth on the second line.

   If you have used any other name during your lifetime, show it on the third line. Do not include nicknames unless used offically at school or work. More than one such name can be shown.

2. Enter the address where you want your Social Security card mailed. If mail under your name is not normally received at the address which you show, use an "in care of" address. **Example: c/o J. Doe, 1 Elm St.**

3. Check the block which applies to you. If you checked "other," please submit a statement explaining your situation and why you need a Social Security number. (You may attach a separate sheet.)

5. See page 4 for more information about this question.

7. Enter your age as of your **last** birthday. If less than 1 year old, enter "0".

8. Enter the city and State where you were born. If you were born outside the U.S., show the name of the city and country. Please do not use abbreviations.

9. Enter your mother's full name at her birth. If your father's last name is different from your name at birth, please explain by writing, for example, "step-father" or "adopted father" after your father's name. If you have ever requested a card before, use the name of the same father, step-father, etc. you used when you first applied.

10. If the individual in Item 1 has applied for a Social Security card before but needs a revised or replacement card, check "Yes" in 10a and complete 10b - 10e. If the date of birth shown in Item 6 is different than the date given on any previous application for a Social Security number card, enter the previously used date of birth in 10e.

    If the individual in Item 1 never applied for a Social Security card before, check "No" in 10a and go to Item 11.

    If the individual in Item 1 doesn't know if he /she ever applied for a Social Security card before, check "Don't Know" in 10a and go to Item 11.

12. Enter a phone number where we can reach you or leave a message for you. Include the area code.

13. Sign your name as it is usually written. Do not print unless your usual signature is printed. If you are applying on behalf of someone else, sign your own name. If you cannot write your name, you may sign by an "X" mark. Two persons must sign as witnesses to your mark.

14. Check the block marked "Self" if you are completing the form for yourself. If you are completing the form for someone else, check the "Other" block and show your relationship; for example, "father" or "guardian."

DEPARTMENT OF HEALTH AND HUMAN SERVICES
SOCIAL SECURITY ADMINISTRATION

Form Approved
OMB No 0960-0066

FORM SS-5 – APPLICATION FOR A SOCIAL SECURITY NUMBER CARD (Original, Replacement or Correction)

Unless the requested information is provided, we may not be able to issue a Social Security Number (20 CFR 422-103(b))

INSTRUCTIONS TO APPLICANT ▶ Before completing this form, please read the instructions on the opposite page. Type or print, using pen with dark blue or black ink. Do not use pencil. SEE PAGE 1 FOR REQUIRED EVIDENCE.

1

NAA — NAME TO BE SHOWN ON CARD: First | Middle | Last

NAB — FULL NAME AT BIRTH (IF OTHER THAN ABOVE): First | Middle | Last

ONA — OTHER NAME(S) USED

2

STT — MAILING ADDRESS (Street/Apt. No., P.O. Box, Rural Route No.)

CTY — CITY (Do not abbreviate) | STE — STATE | ZIP — ZIP CODE

3 CSP — CITIZENSHIP (Check one only)
- ☐ a. U.S. citizen
- ☐ b. Legal alien allowed to work
- ☐ c. Legal alien not allowed to work
- ☐ d. Other (See instructions on Page 2)

4 SEX — SEX
- ☐ MALE
- ☐ FEMALE

5 ETB — RACE/ETHNIC DESCRIPTION (Check one only) (Voluntary)
- ☐ a. Asian, Asian-American or Pacific Islander (Includes persons of Chinese, Filipino, Japanese, Korean, Samoan, etc., ancestry or descent)
- ☐ b. Hispanic (Includes persons of Chicano, Cuban, Mexican or Mexican-American, Puerto Rican, South or Central American, or other Spanish ancestry or descent)
- ☐ c. Negro or Black (not Hispanic)
- ☐ d. Northern American Indian or Alaskan Native
- ☐ e. White (not Hispanic)

6 DOB — DATE OF BIRTH ▶ MONTH | DAY | YEAR

7 AGE — PRESENT AGE

8 PLB — PLACE OF BIRTH ▶ CITY (Do not abbreviate) | STATE OR FOREIGN COUNTRY (Do not abbreviate) | FCI ☐

9

MNA — MOTHER'S NAME AT HER BIRTH: First | Middle | Last (Her maiden name)

FNA — FATHER'S NAME: First | Middle | Last

10 PNO

a. Has a Social Security number card ever been requested for the person listed in item 1? ☐ YES(2) ☐ NO(1) ☐ Don't know(1)

b. Was a card received for the person listed in item 1? ☐ YES(3) ☐ NO(1) ☐ Don't know(1)

▶ IF YOU CHECKED YES TO A OR B, COMPLETE ITEMS C THROUGH E; OTHERWISE GO TO ITEM 11.

SSN — c. Enter the Social Security number assigned to the person listed in item 1. ☐☐☐–☐☐–☐☐☐☐

NLC — d. Enter the name shown on the most recent Social Security card issued for the person listed in item 1.

PDB — e. Date of birth correction (See Instruction 10 on page 2) ▶ MONTH | DAY | YEAR

11 DON — TODAY'S DATE ▶ MONTH | DAY | YEAR

12 Telephone number where we can reach you during the day. Please include the area code. ▶ HOME | OTHER

ASD — **WARNING: Deliberately furnishing (or causing to be furnished) false information on this application is a crime punishable by fine or imprisonment, or both.**

IMPORTANT REMINDER: WE CANNOT PROCESS THIS APPLICATION WITHOUT THE REQUIRED EVIDENCE. SEE PAGE 1.

13 YOUR SIGNATURE

14 YOUR RELATIONSHIP TO PERSON IN ITEM 1: ☐ Self ☐ Other (Specify) ____________

WITNESS (Needed only if signed by mark "X") | WITNESS (Needed only if signed by mark "X")

DO NOT WRITE BELOW THIS LINE (FOR SSA USE ONLY)

DTC (SSA RECEIPT DATE)	NPN		DOC
NTC	CAN	BIC	IDN

ITV ☐ MANDATORY IN PERSON INTERVIEW CONDUCTED

TYPE(S) OF EVIDENCE SUBMITTED

SIGNATURE AND TITLE OF EMPLOYEE(S) REVIEWING EVIDENCE AND/OR CONDUCTING INTERVIEW

DATE

DATE

DCL

Form SS-5 (11-86)
5/84, 1/85 and 8/85 editions may be used until supply is exhausted

THE PRIVACY ACT AND YOUR REQUEST FOR A SOCIAL SECURITY NUMBER CARD

Before we can give you a Social Security number, there is certain information we need from you. The Privacy Act of 1974 and the Paperwork Reduction Act of 1980 require us to give you the following facts when we ask for this information:

- Why the information is needed
- The legal authority for asking for it
- The information you are required to give
- The effects of not providing the information
- How the information will be used and to whom it may be disclosed

Why Information Is Needed

Your Social Security number is needed for us to keep a correct record of your earnings while you are working. It will also be needed if you die, retire or become disabled so that you or your survivors can receive benefits.

The information we request from you is necessary for us to:

- Assign you a Social Security number
- Issue you a replacement card if you lose your card
- Change information on your Social Security record
- Establish and maintain a record of your earnings, and
- Conduct research programs in income distribution and maintenance and health insurance.

Legal Authority to Collect Information

Section 205(c) of the Social Security Act authorizes us to collect the information needed to assign you a Social Security number and issue you a card. Section 702 of the Social Security Act authorizes us to collect the racial/ethnic information needed for statistical purposes.

Required Information

We need the following information to assure that the record we establish for you is your unique and individual record. Specifically, we need your:

- Name as you use it now
- Name at birth
- Place of birth
- Citizenship or alien status
- Date of birth
- Sex
- Mother's name at her birth
- Father's name
- Mailing address
- Signature

We also need to know if you have ever had a Social Security number.

Effects of Withholding Information

You have a right to refuse to give most kinds of information, but usually it is to your advantage to give us the information we ask for. Without it, we will be unable to keep an accurate record of your earnings under Social Security. This could possibly cause you to lose benefits in the future. In some cases, we cannot even give you a number without the information. This could mean you would be unable to get a job, since in most cases you need a number to work.

Disclosure of Information

Sometimes we must disclose information from our records without your written consent. This is done, however, only when necessary and when it is authorized by the law or regulations.

If you would like more information about your rights to privacy, ask any Social Security office for a copy of "Collection and Use of Information by the Social Security Administration" (Form SSA-5000).

Information Concerning Collection of Racial/Ethnic Information

The categories for race and ethnic background have been established by the Office of Federal Statistical Policy and Standards to assure uniform reporting to all Federal agencies. The categories are:

Asian or Pacific Islander

Persons having origins (ancestry) in any of the original peoples of the Far East, Southeast Asia, the Indian subcontinent, or the Pacific Islands. This area includes, for example, China, India, Japan, the Philippine Islands, Korea, Samoa, etc.

Hispanic

Persons of Mexican, Puerto Rican, Cuban, Central or South American, or other Spanish culture or origin (ancestry), regardless of race.

Black or Negro (not Hispanic)

Persons having origins (ancestry) in any of the black racial groups of Africa.

American Indian or Alaskan Native

Persons having origins (ancestry) in any of the original peoples of North America and who maintain cultural identification through tribal affiliation or community recognition.

White (not Hispanic)

Persons having origins (ancestry) in any of the original peoples of Europe, North Africa, or the Middle East.

If you are of mixed racial/ethnic background, choose the category with which you most closely identify yourself.

Completion of Question 5.

While your failure to complete this question will not affect your obtaining a Social Security number, this information is important to find out how Social Security programs affect different groups of people in our Nation. It is also essential for preparing statistics to determine compliance with Federal civil rights laws. When used for this purpose, statistics are presented as summaries or other forms of information which do not reveal the names of individuals.

© U.S. GOVERNMENT PRINTING OFFICE: 1987-196-737

APPENDIX 2

WHERE RECORDS ARE KEPT

For every birth, death, marriage, or divorce, an official document or certificate should be on file in the place (city, county, borough, etc.) where the event occurred. These documents are prepared by authorized persons in each State. Even though the various State laws differ, all States, including the District of Columbia maintain permanent records of these events. The Federal Government does not maintain vital statistics records, but does keep files on the deceased's Social Security numbers.

To obtain a certified copy of a certificate write or go to the Vital Statistics office in the State where the event occurred. Because of recent changes, some vital statistics offices now require personal information from the applicant prior to issuing a certificate. If requesting certificates by mail, the following information should be included:

1. Full name of the person whose record is being requested
2. Sex and race
3. Parents' names, including mother's maiden name
4. Day, month and year of the birth and/or death
5. City of birth or death
6. Purpose for which copy is required
7. Relationship of applicant to the person whose record is requested

As can be seen, the well-prepared persecuted male should have no difficulities in providing all of the necessary information to obtain any needed, certified document. In fact, these recently adopted regulations help weed out the unprepared amateurs only. This in effect enhances the security of those residing in a fade!

The copy fees listed herein are subject to change and should be verified before requesting a certificate.

ALABAMA

Birth and death records
Division of Vital Statistics
State Department of Health
Montgomery, Alabama 36130

Records since 1908.
Copies $3.00.

Marriage records
Address same as above
Before Aug. 1936, those records were available from the probate judge where the license was issued

Divorce records
Address same as above
Before 1950, those records were available from the Court of Equity clerk or Registrar in the County where the divorce was granted.

ALASKA

Birth and death records
Vital Statistics Bureau, Room 115
Alaska Office Building, Pouch H-03
Juneau, Alaska 99811

Since 1913

Copies: $3.00.

Marriage records
Same address as above

Divorce records
Same address as above (since 1950)

Before 1950, Superior Court Clerk, Judicial District where the divorce was granted

Juneau and Ketchikan (1st District)
Nome (2nd District)
Anchorage (3rd District)
Fairbanks (4th District)

AMERICAN SAMOA

Birth and death records
Office of the Territorial Registrar
Government of American Samoa
Pago Pago, Samoa 96799

Records since 1900

Copies $1.00.

ARIZONA

Birth and death records
Vital Records Section, Department of Health Services
P.O. Box 3887
Phoenix, AZ 85030

Records since 1909

Copies $2.00.

Marriage records
Superior Court Clerk, County where license was issued

Divorce records
Superior Court Clerk where divorce was granted

ARKANSAS

Birth and death records
Division of Vital Records
Arkansas Department of Health
4815 West Markham Street
Little Rock, Arkansas 72201

Before Feb. 1914
Arkansas Historical Commission
State Capitol Mall
Little Rock, Arkansas 72201

Copies $3.00.

Marriage records
Address same as above
Before 1917, County Clerk where license was issued.

Divorce records
Address same as above
Before 1923, County or Chancery Court Clerk, County where the divorce was granted

CALIFORNIA

Birth and death records
Vital Statistics Branch, Department of Health Services
410 N Street
Sacramento, CA 95814
Records since July, 1905

Before July 1905, County Recorder or City Health Office, or city where the event occured

Copies $2.00.

Marriage records
Address same as above

Divorce Records
Address same as above

Before 1962, Superior Court Clerk, County where divorce grant ed

CANAL ZONE

Birth and death records
Vital Statistics Clerk, Health Bureau
Balboa Heights, Canal Zone
Records since May, 1904.

Copies $2.00.

COLORADO

Birth and death records
Records and Statistics Section, Department of Health
4210 East 11th Avenue
Denver, Colorado 80220

Death records since 1900
Birth records since 1910

Copies $2.00.

Marriage records
Address same as above, or County Clerk where license issued.

Divorce records
Before 1940, and since 1967, address same as above. From 1940 to 1967, District or County Clerk where divorce granted

CONNECTICUT

Birth and death records
Since July 1897, Public Health Statistics Section
State Department of Health
79 Elm Street
Hartford, Connecticut 06115

Before July 1897, Registrar of Vital Statistics, town where event occured

Copies $2.00.

Marriage records
Address same as above, information same as above

Divorce records
Since 1935, Superior Court where divorce granted

Before 1935, Head Clerk of Court, Courthouse where the divorce granted

DELAWARE

Birth and death records
Bureau of Vital Statistics, Division of Public Health and Social Services
Jesse S. Cooper Memorial Building
Dover, Delaware 19901

Copy $2.50.

Marriage records
Address same as above

Divorce records
Since 1970 address same as above

Before 1970, Head Clerk of Court
County where divorce granted

DISTRICT OF COLUMBIA

Birth and death records
Bureau of Vital Statistics
300 Indiana Avenue NW, Washington, D.C. 2001

Copy $1.00.

Marriage records
Clerk of Superior Court
Building A, Room 111
505 Fifth Street NW, Washington, D.C. 2001

Divorce records
Since Sept. 16, 1956, Clerk, Superior Court for the District of Columbia, Family Division
500 Indiana Avenue NW, Washington D.C. 2001

Before Sept. 16, 1956, Clerk, U.S. District Court for the District of Columbia, Washington D.C. 2001

FLORIDA

Birth and death records
Department of Health and Rehabilitative Services
P.O. Box 210
Jacksonville, Florida 32231

Birth records since April 1865

Some death records prior to January 1917
Complete records since 1917

Copy $2.00.

Marriage records
Since June 6, 1927, address same as above

Before June 6, 1927 Circuit Court Clerk, County where license issued

Divorce records
Since June 6, 1927, address same as above

Before June 6, 1927, Circuit Court Clerk
County where divorce was granted

GEORGIA

Birth and death record
Vital Records Service
State Department of Human Resources, Room 217-H
47 Trinity Avenue SW
Atlanta, Georgia 30334

Records since January 1, 1917

Before January 1, 1917 County Health Department where birth or death occured

Copy $3.00.

Marriage records
Since June 9, 1952, address same as above

Before June 9, 1952 County Financial Officer
County where license was issued

Divorce records
Since 1952, address same as above

Before 1952, Superior Court Clerk, County where the divorce granted

GUAM

Birth and death records
Office of Vital Statistics, Department of Public Health and Social Services
Government of Guam
P.O. Box 2816
Agana, Guam M.I. 96910

Records since October 26, 1901

Copy $1.00

HAWAII

Birth and death records
Research and Statistics Office, State Department of Health
P.O. Box 3378
Honolulu, Hawaii

Records since 1853

Copies $2.00

Marriage records
Address same as above

Divorce records
Since July 1951, address same as above. Before July, 1951, Circuit Court, County where the divorce was granted

IDAHO

Birth and death records
Bureau of Vital Statistics, State Department of Health and Welfare
Statehouse
Boise, Idaho 83720

Records since 1911
From 1907 to 1911 County Recorder where birth/death occurred

Copy $2.00.

Marriage records
Since 1947, address same as above

Before 1947, County Recorder, County where license was issued.

Divorce records
Since 1947, address same as above.
Before 1947, County Recorder, County where divorce granted

ILLINOIS

Birth and death records
Since 1916, Office of Vital Records, State Department of Pub
lic Health
535 West Jefferson Street
Springfield, Ohio 62761

Before 1916 County Clerk, County where event occured

Copy $3.00

Marriage records
Since 1962, address same as above

Before 1962, County Clerk, County where license issued

INDIANA

Birth and death records
Births since Oct. 1907, deaths since 1900
Division of Vital Records
State Board of Health
1330 West Michigan Street
Indianapolis, Indiana 46202

Births before Oct. 1907, and deaths before 1900,
Health Officer, City or County where event occurred

Copy $3.00

Marriage records
Since 1958 address same as above
Before 1958, Circuit or Superior Court Clerk
County where license was issued

Divorce records
Address same as above
County Clerk, County where divorce granted

IOWA

Birth and death records
Vital Records Section, State Department of Health
Lucas Building
Des Moines, Iowa 50319

Records since July 1, 1880

Copy $3.00

Marriage records
Address same as above

Divorce records
Since 1906, same address as above.

Before 1906, County Clerk, County where divorce granted

KANSAS

Birth and death records
Since July, 1911, Department of Health and Enviroment, Vital Statistics
Topeka, Kansas 66620

Before July, 1911, County Clerk, County where event occurred

Copy $2.00

Marriage records
Since July 1913, address same as above

Before May, 1913, District Court Marriage License Clerk County where license was obtained

Divorce records
Since July, 1951, same address as above

Before July 1951, Clerk of District Court where divorce granted

KENTUCKY

Birth and death records
Since July, 1911, Office of Vital Statistics
275 East Main Street
Frankfort, Kentucky 40621

Before Jan. 1911, Historical Society
3016 P.O. Box H
Frankfort, Kentucky 40621

Copies $2.00

Marriage records Since July, 1958, address same as above
Before July 1958, County Court Clerk, County where license issued

Death records address and conditions same as above

LOUISIANA

Birth and death records
Since July 1914m Office of Vital Records
P.O. Box 60630
New Orleans, Louisiana 70160

Before July 1914 Parish Clerk, parish where event occurred.
New Orleans, since 1790, address same as above

Copies $2.00

Marriage records
Since 1946, address same as above
Before 1946, Court Clerk, Parrish where license issued

New Orleans since 1831, address same as above

Divorce records
Same address and conditions as above

New Orleans, Civil District Court
421 Loyola Avenue
New Orleans, Louisiana 70112

MAINE

Birth and death records
Since 1892, Office of Vital Statistics
State Department of Human Services
State House, Augusta, Maine 04333

Before 1892, Town Clerk, town where the event occurred

Copies $2.00.

Marriage records
Address same as above, or local office where intentions were filed

Divorce Records
Since 1892, address same as above

Before 1892, Superior Court Clerk
County where the divorce granted, or District Court Clerk
Judicial Division where the divorce granted

MARYLAND

<u>Birth and death records</u>
Division of Vital Records, Department of Health and Mental Hygiene
Herbert R. O'Conor Building
201 West Preston Street
P.O. Box 13146
Baltimore, Maryland 21201

Records since 1898. Records for Baltimore since 1875

<u>Marriage records</u> since June, 1951 address same as above
Before June, 1951, Clerk of Circuit Court, County where marriage occurred

<u>Divorce records</u>
Since June, 1961, Division of Vital Records
P.O. Box 18146
Baltimore, Maryland 21203

Before June, 1961 Clerk of Circuit Court, County where divorce granted

MASSACHUSETTS

<u>Birth and death records</u>
Since 1841, Registrar of Vital Statistics
McCormack Building
1 Ashburton Place
Boston, Massachusetts 02108

Before 1841, Clerk, city or town where the event occurred

Boston, City Registrar, Registry Division
Health Department, Room 705
1 City Hall Square
Boston, Massachusetts 02201

Copies $2.00.

<u>Marriage records</u>
address same as above
Boston, same address as above

<u>Divorce records</u>
Superior Court Clerk or Registrar of probate
county where the divorce was granted
Boston, same address as above

MICHIGAN

<u>Birth and death records</u>
Office of Vital and Health Statistics
Department of Public Health
3500 North Logan Street
P.O. Box 30035
Lansing, Michigan 48909

or County Clerk where event occurred

Copies $2.00

<u>Marriage records</u>
Address same as above

<u>Divorce records</u>
Address same as above

MINNESOTA

<u>Birth and death records</u>
Since 1908, Minnesota Department of Health
Section of Vital Statistics
717 Delaware Street SE
Minneapolis, Minnesota 55440

Before 1908, District Court Clerk, County where event occurred

Minneapolis and St. Paul, City Health Departments

<u>Marriage record</u>
Since 1958, address same as above

Before 1958, District Court Clerk, County where license issued

<u>Divorce records</u>
Since 1970, address same as above

Before 1970, District Court Clerk, County where divorce granted

MISSISSIPPI

<u>Birth and death records</u>
Vital Records Registration Unit, State Board of Health
P.O. Box 1700
Jackson, Mississippi 39205

Copies $2.00

Marriage records
Since 1926 (excluding period July 1, 1938-Dec. 31,1941), ad dress same as above

Before 1926, and for the period of July 1, 1938 to Dec. 31, 1941, Circuit Clerk, County where license issued

Divorce records
Chancery Clerk, County where the divorce granted

MISSOURI

Birth and death records
Since Jan. 1, 1910 Vital Records
Division of Health
P.O. Box 570
Jefferson City, Missouri 65101

Copies $2.00

Marriage records
Since July 1948, address same as above

Before July, 1948, Recorder of Deeds, County where license is sued

Divorce records
Since July, 1948, address same as above

Before July, 1948, Circuit Court Clerk, County where divorce granted

MONTANA

Birth and death records
Bureau of Records and Statistics, State Department of Health and Enviroment Sciences
Helena, Montana 59601

Copies $2.00

Marriage records
Since 1943, address same as above

Before 1943, District Court Clerk, County where license issued

Divorce records
Since 1943, address same as above

Before 1943

District Court Clerk, County where divorce granted

NEBRASKA

<u>Birth and death records</u>
Since 1904, Bureau of Vital Statistics
State Deparment of Health
301 Centennial Mall South
P.O. Box 95007
Lincoln, Nebraska 68509

Before 1904, Division of Vital Statistics
Omaha/Douglas County Health Department
Civic Center
1819 Farnam
Omaha, Nebraska 68102

Copies $3.00

<u>Marriage records</u>
Since 1909, address same as above

Before 1909, County Court, County where license issued

<u>Divorce records</u>
Since 1909, address same as above

Before 1909, Clerk of District Court where the divorce granted

NEVADA

<u>Birth and death records</u>
Since July 1911, Department of Human Resources
Division of Health
Section of Vital Statistics
Capitol Complex
Carson City, Nevada 89710

Before July 1911, County Recorder, County where event occurred

Copies $2.00

<u>Marriage records</u>
Since Jan, 1968, address same as above

Before Jan, 1968, County Recorder, County where license issued

<u>Divorce records</u>
Address and conditions same as marriage records, above

NEW HAMPSHIRE

<u>Birth and death records</u>
Division of Public Health Services
Bureau of Vital Records and Health Statistics
Health and Welfare Building
Hazen Drive
Concord, New Hamshire 03301

Copies $2.00

<u>Marriage records</u>
Address same as above

<u>Divorce records</u>
Address same as above, or Clerk of Superior Court where decree issued

NEW JERSEY

<u>Birth and death records</u>
Since June, 1878, State Department of Health
Bureau of Vital Statistics
P.O. Box 1540
Trenton, New Jersey 08625

1848 to May 1878, State Archives

Copies $2.00

<u>Marriage records</u>
Address same as above

<u>Divorce records</u>
Clerk, Superior Court
State House Annex
P.O. Box 1300
Trenton, New Jersey 08625
Att: Matrimonial Unit

NEW MEXICO

<u>Birth and Death records</u>
Vital Statistics Bureau
Health and Environmental Department
P.O. Box 968,
PERA Building, Room 118
Santa Fe, New Mexico 87503

Copies $2.00

Marriage records
County Clerk, County where marriage performed

Divorce Records
District Court Clerk, County where divorce granted

NEW YORK

Birth and death records
Bureau of Vital Records
State Department of Health
Albany, New York 12237

Copies $2.00

New York City
Bureau of Records and Statistics
Borough where the event occurred

Copies $3.00

Marriage records
1880-1907 and since May, 1915, Bureau of Vital Records
State Department of Health
Albany, New York 12237

1908-Apr. 1915. County Clerk, County where license issued

New York City, since May 13, 1943, City Clerks office where license issued

1908-May 12, 1943, City Clerk's office in Borough of bride

Non-residents, City Clerks Office where license obtained

Divorce records
Since 1963, Bureau of Vital Records
State Department of Health
Albany, New York 12237

Before 1963, County Clerk, County where divorce granted

New York, City Borough of Court where divorce granted

NORTH CAROLINA

Birth and death records
Since Oct. 1, 1913, Vital Records Branch
Division of Health Services
P.O. Box 2091
Raleigh, North Carolina 27602

Copies $2.00

Marriage records
Since 1962, address same as above

Before 1962, Register of Deeds, County where marriage per formed

Divorce records
Since 1958, address same as above

Before 1958, Superior Court Clerk, County where divorce grant ed

NORTH DAKOTA

Birth and death records
Division of Vital Records
State Department of Health
State Capitol
Bismark, North Dakota 58505

Copies $2.00

Marriage records
Since July 1925, address same as above

Before July 1925, County Judge, County where license issued

Divorce records
Since July 1949, address same as above

Before July 1949, District Court Clerk, County where divorce granted

OHIO

Birth and death records
Since Dec. 20, 1908, Division of Vital Statistics
State Department of Health
G-20 State Departments Building
65 South Front Street, Columbus, Ohio 43215

Before Dec. 20, 1908, Probate Court, County where event oc curred

Copies $1.00

OKLAHOMA

<u>Birth and death records</u>
Vital Records Division
Oklahoma State Department of Health
1000 NE 10th Street
P.O. Box 5355
Oklahoma City, Oklahoma 73152

Copies $2.00

<u>Marriage records</u>
Court Clerk, County where license issued

<u>Divorce records</u>
Court Clerk, County where divorce granted

OREGON

<u>Birth and death records</u>
Vital Statistics Section
Oregon State Health Division
P.O. Box 231
Portland, Oregon 97207

Copies $3.00

<u>Marriage records</u>
Since 1906, address same as above

Before 1906, County Clerk, County where license issued

<u>Divorce records</u>
Since 1925, address same as above

Before 1925, County Clerk, County where divorce granted

PENNSYLVANIA

<u>Birth and death records</u>
Since 1906, Division of Vital Statistics
P.O. Box 1528
New Castle, Pennsylvania 16103

Before 1906, Register of Wills, Orphan's Court, County where event occurred

Marriage records
Marriage license Clerk, County seat where license issued

Divorce records
Head Clerk of Court, County Courthouse
County Seat where divorce granted

PUERTO RICO

Birth and death records
Since July 22, 1931, Division of Demographic Registry and Vital Statistics
Department of Health
San Juan, Puerto Rico 00908

Before July 22 1931, Local Registrar (Registrador Demografico) in the municipality or to central office where event occurred

Copies $0.50

RHODE ISLAND

Birth and death records
Division of Vital Statistics
State Department of Health, Room 101
Health Building
Davis Street
Providence, Rhode Island 02908

Before 1953, Town Clerk, town where event occurred

Marriage records
Since 1636, address same as above

Before 1936, Rhode Island Historical Society
110 Benevolent Street
Providence, Thode Island 02906

Divorce records
Family Court of Rhode Island
22 Hays Street
Providence, Rhode Island 02908,

or,

Family Court Clerk, County where divorce granted

SOUTH CAROLINA

Birth and death records
Office of Vital Records
South Carolina Department of Health and Environmental Control
Sims Building
Columbia, South Carolina 29201

Before 1915, County Health Department
County where event occurred

Copies $2.00

Marriage records
Since July 1950, address same as above

July 1911-June 1950, Probate Judge, County where license is sued

Divorce records
Since July 1962, address same as above

Apr. 1949-June 1962, County Clerk, County where petition filed

SOUTH DAKOTA

Birth and death records
Public Health Statistics
State Department of Health
Joe Foss Building
Pierre, South Dakota 57501

Copies $2.00

Marriage records
Since 1905, address same as above

Before 1905, County Treasurer, County where license issued

Divorce records
Conditions and address same as marriage records

TENNESSEE

Birth and death records
Vital Records
State Department of Public Health
C3-324 Cordell Hull Building
Nashville, Tennessee 37219

Copies $2.00

Marriage records
Since July 1945, address same as above

Before July 1945, County Court Clerk, County where license issued

Divorce records
Conditions and address same as marriage records

TEXAS

Birth and death records
Bureau of Vital Statistics
Texas Department of Health
1100 West 49th Street
Austin, Texas 78756

Copies $2.00.

Marriage records
Since Jan. 1966, address same as above

Before Jan. 1966, County Clerk, County where license issued

Divorce records
Conditions and address same as marriage records

TERRITORY OF PACIFIC ISLANDS

All records, Director of Medical Services
Department of Medical Services
Saipan, Mariana Islands 96950

Or,

Clerk of Court, District where event occurred

UTAH

Birth and death records
Since 1905, Utah State Division of Health
Bureau of Health Statistics
150 West North Temple
P.O. Box 2500
Salt Lake City 84110

Before 1905, County Clerk, County where event occurred

Or,

Salt Lake City and Ogden Boards of Health

Copies $11.00

Marriage records
County Clerk, County where license issued

Divorce records
District Court Clerk, County where divorce granted

VERMONT

Birth and death records
Since 1955, Public Health Statistics
Vermont Department of Health
115 Colchester Avenue
Burlington, Vermont 05401

Before 1955, Public Records Division
Adminstration Department
133 State Street
Montpelier, Vermont 05602
Copies $2.00.

Marriage records
Since 1955, address same as above

Before, address same as above
1857-1954 address same as above
Before 1857, Town Clerk, town where license issued

Divorce records
Since 1968, address same as above

1860-1967,Public Records Division
Administration Department
133 State Street
Montpelier, Vermont 05602

Before 1860, County Court, County where divorce granted

VIRGINIA

Birth and death records
1853-1896, and since June 14, 1912
Bureau of Vital Records and Health Statistics
State Department of Health
Madison Building
P.O. Box 1000
Richmond, Virginia 23208

1897-June 13,1912
Health Department
City where event occurred

Copies $2.00

<u>Marriage records</u>
Since 1853, address same as above

Before 1853, Court Clerk
County or City where license issued

<u>Divorce records</u>
Since 1918, address same as above

Before 1918, Court Clerk
County or City where divorce granted

VIRGIN ISLANDS (St. Thomas)

All records, birth and death, since 1906
Registrar of Vital Statistics
Charlotte Amalie
St. Thomas, Virgin Islands 00802

Copies $2.00

VIRGIN ISLANDS (St. Croix)

All records, birth and death, since 1840
Registrar of Vital Statistics
Charles Harwood Memorial Hospital
St. Croix, Virgin Islands

Copies $2.00

WASHINGTON

<u>Birth and death records</u>
Since July 1907, Vital Records
P.O. Box 9709
Olympia, Washington 98504

Before July 1907, Auditor, County where event occurred

Copies $3.00

<u>Marriage records</u>
Since 1968, address same as above

Before 1968, County Auditor
County where license issued

Divorce records
Since 1968, address same as above

Before 1968, County Clerk
County where divorce granted

WEST VIRGINIA

Birth and death records
Since 1917, State Registrar of Vital Statistics
State Capitol Building
Charleston, West Virginia 25305

Before 1917, County Court Clerk, C

VIRGIN ISLANDS (St. Thomas)

All records, birth and death, since 1906
Registrar of Vital Statistics
Charlotte Amalie
St. Thomas, Virgin Islands 00802

Copies $2.00

VIRGIN ISLANDS (St. Croix)

All records, birth and death, since 1840
Registrar of Vital Statistics
Charles Harwood Memorial Hospital
St. Croix, Virgin Islands

Copies $2.00

WASHINGTON

Birth and death records
Since July 1907, Vital Records
P.O. Box 9709
Olympia, Washington 98504

Before July 1907, Auditor, County where the event occurred

Copies $3.00

Marriage records
Since 1968, address same as above

Before 1968, County Auditor
County where the license was issued

Divorce records
Since 1968, address same as above

Before 1968, County Clerk
County where the divorce was granted.

WEST VIRGINIA

Birth and death records
Since 1917, State Registrar of Vital Statistics
State Capitol Building
Charleston, West Virginia 25305

Before 1917, County Court Clerk, County where event occurred

Copies $1.00

Marriage records
Since 1921, address same as above

Before 1921, County Clerk, County where license issued

Divorce records
Circuit Court Clerk, Chancery Side, County where divorce granted

WISCONSIN

Birth and death records
Some records since 1814; early records are incomplete
Section of Vital Records
Division of Health
P.O. Box 309
Madison, Wisconsin 53701

Copies $4.00

Marriage records, address same as above

Divorce records, address same as above

WYOMING

Birth and death records
Since 1909, Vital Records Services
Division of Health and Medical Services
Hathaway Building
Cheyenne, Wyoming 82002

Before 1909, State Archives

Copies $2.00

Marriage records
Since May 1941, address same as above

Before May 1941, County Clerk, County where license issued

Divorce records
Since May 1941, address same as above

Before May 1941, District Court Clerk
County where divorce granted

APPENDIX 3

DRIVERS LICENSE AND ID CARD DATA

The Drivers License was originally intended to provide its owner with proof of proficiency in operating a motor vehicle, and knowing and abiding by the rules of the road. Today, the drivers' license is also accepted a the primary means of personal identification. Drivers' licenses are issued by all fifty States and the District of Columbia.

Because of the widespread usage of the drivers' license for personal identification, most States are taking steps to make them more secure from potential abuse. The use of counterfeit and altered licenses has necessitated the use of tamper-resistant, hard-to-recreate types of material. The old, easy-to-alter cardboard style is being gradually replaced by the difficult-to-duplicate, photographic type. A few remaining States still use a data processing card for their permanent license. These licenses are the prime target for counterfeiters and those desiring to alter the data contained on them.

At one time, some States were requiring fingerprints of the licensee on the format of their drivers license. At the present, no State uses this provision. California asks for voluntary fingerprints on its drivers licenses and I.D. cards but this request is usually declined by those seeking privacy.

There are several States that still don't use a photograph of the licensee. In the United States, these are: Maine, Mississippi (both types), New Jersey (both types), New York, Tennessee, Vermont (both types), and Wisconsin. In Canada, non-photo licenses are used by Manitoba, New Brunswick, New Foundland, Nova Scotia, Ontario, Quebec, Saskatchewan, and the North West Territories. A photoless drivers' license is often used for assuming another's identity. The drivers Social Security number is still being used by some States, but its use has been outlawed by the Privacy Act which states that it is illegal to use the Social Security number on the Drivers' License after January 1, 1975.

The National Driver Register (N.D.R.) located in Washington, D.C. is a National Agency serving as an information exchange. The Agency's primary function is to maintain nationwide records on licensees who have had their license revoked or suspended. The purpose is to prevent these drivers from obtaining a license in another State. The N.D.R. is an information exchange only, and has no enforcment authority; this is left to the individual States.

The N.D.R. <u>is</u> <u>not</u> available to the provinces of Canada.

The N.D.R. lists approximately eleven million names of licensees with clouded drivers' records. Thousands more are added each week. The Agency's computers can respond to over 100,000 inquiries each day. The computers are also programmed (wild card option) to flag those licensees who change or rearrange their date of birth, or alter the order of their names.

Those individuals in the process of fading (or already in a fade) who have properly prepared themselves will be invisible to these efforts.

The Uniform Vehicle Code, the Highway Safety Program #5, and the Drivers' License Compact are the results of various State Agencies to standardize and share motor vehicle information (drivers license and vehicle registration) with one another. The members of these organizations all recommend confiscation of an applicant's old out-of-State license and returning it to the issuing State before a new license is issued. These compacts are being phased out in favor of the NDR.

Some States still do not confiscate an out-of-State license when issuing a new one, thus allowing the licensee to hold two valid drivers licenses. At last report, these were: Connecticut, Iowa, New Jersey, Vermont, and Washington. A few States simply destroy the out-of-State license if a new one is issued without notifying anyone. These States are ideal selections for those entering a fade; there are no paper tracks! If, for example, a licensee was to change his name by the "use" method, and then apply for a new license in one of these liberal States, the original State would never be notified of the move or change of name.

An "International Drivers License" is issued by the American Automobile Association (AAA) and may be legally used world wide. Qualifications are: a valid State drivers' license and two passport-type photos. No other forms of I.D. are required. The license is generally made while you wait. A $5.00 charge is assessed. Check the "white" pages of the telephone directory for the nearest AAA.

This is indeed one of the situations where the licensee may legally posess more than one drivers license. Only four States require notification when one of their licensees applies for an international drivers license. These are: Arkansas, Idaho, Mississippi and Wyoming. The previous driving records of their licensees are required by only eight states before permitting the AAA to issue an international drivers license. These are: Colorado, District of Columbia, Idaho, Indiana, Kentucky, Mississippi, Tennessee, and Wyoming.
Other than for the few States listed, licensees from all other States can easily obtain an international drivers license which leaves (or creates) virtually no paper tracks.

An international drivers' license is primarily intended for use outside of the United States, but reports insist that large numbers of drivers are successfully using the license inside the U.S. as well, such as the American tourist who lived abroad for years, and only maintained his International license in preference over his State drivers license. The judicial use of the international drivers' license presents numerous possibilities to those in a fade. Some foreign countries will issue an international drivers' license of their own, which also is accepted in the USA.

State laws are constantly being changed by the various legislators. Drivers' license regulations are no exception.
Which states use the N.D.R. or any of the other shared information programs could easily be checked by calling the Department of Motor Vehicles in the selected State. Of particular interest would also be just what becomes of the old drivers license once surrendered?

Even though it may be against the law, there always seems to be a market for well-made counterfeit documents such as drivers' licenses or State I.D. cards. The craftsmen involved in this dubious occupation require samples and coding information from which to work. Some amateurs boast of having achieved remarkable duplications by using home Polaroid cameras and closeup lenses. Self generated documents are far more secure (no one else knows) than purchased ones. Some persecuted males have actually purchased commercial equipment and have manufactured their own documents.

Many States use the Polaroid I.D. system to manufacture their own official drivers licenses and I.D. cards. This equipment is available from Polaroid Corporation, Identification Systems Marketing, 575 Technology Square, Cambridge, Mass., 1-800-225-1618 or 617-547-5177. Call for prices and details. Polaroid claims to be able to produce a perfect I.D. card in less than two minutes.

An excellent source of full color, actual size prints of every States' drivers license is: Drivers License Guide Company, 1492 Oddstad Drive, Redwood, CA 94063, (415) 369-4849. Titled "Drivers' License Guide," this 96 page masterpiece sells for $15.95 plus $1.50 shipping.

The ultimate reference for those truly interested in the intricacies of personal identification is available from the same Company, titled, "U.S. Identification Manual," priced at $99.00 plus $4.00 shipping. This incredible, 700-hundred page manual devotes more than 350 pages to US and Canadian drivers licenses and I.D. cards. All formats are actual size and in full and accurate color. Over two hundred and fifty color pages, including actual size formats display virtually all U.S. and Canadian vehicle registrations.

Other sections accurately display Federal I.D. cards, immigration documents, military I.D., plus Social Security card coding. There is also an excellent section covering over 100 credit cards, including the special coding used. Included in the $99.00 price tag is a full year of updates, usually over 300 pages annually.

The publisher requests that orders be sent on appropriate letterhead or proof of security employment. Some persecuted males report little difficulty in purchasing either manual by generating their own letterhead and using the mail drop system.

The Remington Rand SOUNDEX system is the most commonly used method in coding drivers licenses and State I.D. cards.
In this coding system, a four-character code is developed using the first letter of the surname (last name), and the coded number equivalents for each subsequent non-doubled consonant (a letter which is not a vowel), as shown in the following table:

LETTERS (consonants)	NUMBER EQUIVALENTS
b,f,p,v	1
c,g,j,k,q,s,x,z	2
d,t	3
l	4
m,n	5
r	6

Using the table, the name Morgan would be coded as shown:

1st character M = M First letter of last name
character O = skipped, not in table, hence not counted
2nd character R = 6 from table
3rd character G = 2 from table
4th character A = 0 When insufficient consonants to get 3 add zeros

Thus, the name MORGAN would be coded M620. Using the same table, the name ANDERSON would be coded A536.

After the initial four-character SOUNDEX coding, any additional numbers found on a drivers' license or I.D. card, as many as 15, may represent birth day, month, and year, or an additional SOUNDEX code of first name, middle name, etc. A quick check for a SOUNDEX coded license or I.D. card is matching first letter of last name with first character of license number.

How do police detect a fraudulent or altered drivers' license? What do they look for?

If presented with an in-State license, a call on the radio will provide the officer with license status, and also verify the data and number. As of yet, no known way to verify the photo except by visual comparison with the driver. Any discrepancy would alert the officer to investigate further.

If presented with an out-of-State license, the officer could initiate an on-line data check with the issuing State (if a member of a compact) or the N.D.R.

Most highway patrol officers carry a recent copy of the "Drivers License Guide", or a similiar manual as part of their inventory. Suspected fraudulent, or altered licenses would be examined visually and compared against the manual sample. Officers are trained to look for two types of fraud: alteration of valid licenses, and fraudulent licenses designed closely around the valid license.

The following procedures were borrowed from an actual State Highway Patrol seminar, "Detecting Drivers License Fraud:"

1. Confirm the format against the manual sample.

2. Look for additions. The most commonly used addition is a plastic lamination not applied by the DMV.

3. All photos should be a part of the license format. An edge should not be visible or felt under the lamination.

4. Check the validation against that in the manual. Most counterfeiters fail in this regard. Even stolen license blanks will not have the proper validation markings.

5. Check the license data carefully, then question the individual on this data. Watch for discrepancies between license number code, birth date, and name.

6. If suspicious, take additional time studying license, watch for signs of nervousness in driver behavior. Ask for support I.D., look for documents at least a year, preferably two years old. Most forgers have little support documentation, most of it being new.

7. The drivers license manual provided is extremely accurate in markings and color, the forgery will usually stand out as a fake when compared to the sample.

8. Use the special light (black light) provided to spot erasures, cutting out of data, or overlap of new data.

The following tables will provide a brief description of each State's drivers' license and I.D. card format. Since drivers' license and I.D. card formats are constantly being changed, such data should be used with caution. To use an altered or counterfeit license to establish I.D. could be forgiven, to use one as a drivers license is insanity.

ALABAMA

Description, photographic, enclosed in plastic, Director's signature appears above photo, manufacturing process, Polaroid.

Photo, upper right hand corner, red backdrop.

Verification, State Seal and camera number overlapping LH, photo edge.

License number, up to seven digits, no spacing, not coded.

Police quick check, State Seal overlaps photo.

I.D. card, photographic, format like drivers' license. Has heading "ALABAMA NON DRIVER ID".

ALASKA

Description, photographic, enclosed in plastic, completed in computer or typewriter, manufacturing process, Polaroid.

Photo, Upper left hand corner, yellow backdrop.

Verification, Commissioner's signature overlaps bottom of photo, camera number overlaps photo on RH margin.

License number, up to seven digits, no spacing, not coded.

Police quick check, State Seal overprinted on licensee's signature. Under 19 has red photo backdrop.

I.D. card data, process identical to drivers license, format slightly different. Under 18 has red backdrop, adult yellow. Diagonal bar shows "NOT A DRIVERS' LICENSE."

ARIZONA

Description, photographic, polyester coating on front, license is flexible, not laminated, manufactiromg: DEK/Electro

Photo, lower right hand corner, blue backdrop.

Verification, State Seal on front, director'ss signature on bottom of license.

License number, One or two letters, followed by five or six digits, not coded, seven digits max.

Police quick check, pattern design on face, data may be hand written or typed.

I.D. card data, process identical to drivers license, red letters showing "IDENTIFICATION CARD ONLY."

ARKANSAS

Description, photographic, laminated, manufacturer: Polaroid.

Photo, lower right hand corner, red backdrop.

Verification, State Seal overlaps upper LH corner of photo, director's signature accross top of photo.

License number, seven digit number in sequence, with the 8th digit as a check number. Example 1234-5678

Police quick check, director's signature overlapping on top of photo.
I.D. card data, process identical to driver's license, showing "ARKANSAS IDENTIFICATION CARD."

ARIZONA

Description, photographic, polyester coating on front, flexible, not laminated, mfg., DEC/Electro.

Photo, lower right hand corner, blue backdrop.

Verification, State Seal on front of license, director's sig nature on bottom.

License number, One or two letters, followed by five or six numbers, not coded, seven digits max.

Police quick check, pattern on license stock, data may be typed or hand printed.

I.D. card data, process identical to drivers license, marked in red letters, "IDENTIFICATION CARD ONLY."

ARKANSAS

Description, photographic, laminated, manufacturer: Polaroid.

Photo, lower right hand corner, red backdrop.

Verification, State Seal overlaps upper left hand corner of photo. Camera mumber overlaps photo left side. License color yellow.

License number, seven digit sequential number, 8th digit a check number, as follows: 1234-5678

Police quick check, State Seal on photo corner, director's signature overlaps photo on top.

I.D. card data, process identical to drivers license. Marked "ARKANSAS IDENTIFICATION CARD."

CALIFORNIA

Description, photographic, 3M retro-reflective laminate on front. Has slippery feel to front surface. Mfg. DEK/Electro.

Photo, lower left hand corner, light blue backdrop.

Verification, hidden State Seal and word "California."

License number, One letter and four to seven digits, no spacing, not coded.

Police quick check, hidden Seal, word "California", and any alterations show as breaks in retro-reflective film, visible under flash, or black light.

I. D. card data, process identical as drivers license. Marked in green letters, "CALIFORNIA IDENTIFICATION CARD."

COLORADO

Description, photographic, polycarbonate coating, thin, flexible. Manufacturing: DEC/Electro.

Photo, lower right hand corner, light blue or red backdrop.

Verification, State Seal in center, director's signature in red, bottom center of license.

License number, One to four letters and up to six digits. First letter indicates date of issue, A for 1981, B for 1982, C for 1983, and so on.

Police quick check, under 21 has "P" prefix to number. Under 18 has "M".

I.D. card data, process identical as drivers license. Several types as per age group.

CONNECTICUT

Description, photographic, laminated. Manufacturer: Polaroid.

Photo, full, left hand side, blue backdrop.

Verification, very faint State Seal, director's signature and camera number overlap right hand edge of photo.

License number, Nine digits, no spacing. First digits, 01-12 = month of birth if odd year birth.

Police quick check, director's signature overlaps photo on righthand side.

I.D. card data, none issued.

DELAWARE

Description, photgraphic, laminated. Manufacturer: unknown.

Photo, lower right hand corner, blue backdrop.

Verification, director's signature across top of photo. Fee stamp on bottom. large State Seal, center of license.

License number, One to six digits, not coded.

Police quick check, no raised edges around photo. Date and fee stamped at bottom.

I.D. card data, process identical to drivers license. Marked, "DELAWARE IDENTIFICATION CARD." Format, identical to driver's license.

DISTRICT OF COLUMBIA

Description, photographic, laminated. Manufacturer: Polaroid. Computer dot matrix printer used for printing data.

Photo, upper left hand corner, yellow backdrop.

Verification, director's signature overlapping bottom of photo.

License number, Social Security number, or assigned number.

Police quick check, director's signature overlapping bottom of photo. Check for dot matrix printing style.

I.D. card data, process and format identical to driver's license. Marked, "NON-DRIVER CARD."

FLORIDA

Description, photographic, laminated. Manufacturer: DEK/Electro. May be marked, "VALID FLA ONLY" or "SAFE DRIVER RENEWAL" in place of "LICENSE TYPE." Data lettering in red.

Photo, full, left hand side, blue background.

Verification, small State Seal and camera number overlap right hand edge of photo. Concealed State Seals, visible under black light.

License number, Soundex system. Two-digit group is year of birth.

Police quick check, Black light check or year of birth coded in license number.

I.D. card data, process identical to drivers license. Marked, "STATE OF FLORIDA IDENTIFICATION CARD," in red/orange heading.

GEORGIA

Description, photographic, laminated. Manufacturer: DEK/Electro.

Photo, lower right hand corner, blue backdrop.

Verification, Commissioner's and Governor's signatures plus State Seal. State outline in center of license.

License number, up to nine digits, not coded. Social Security number may be used.

Police quick check, wavy lines over lower half of State outline.

I.D. card data, process identical to drivers license. Marked, "GEORGIA IDENTIFICATION CARD."

HAWAII

Description, photographic, plastic card, similar to credit cards. Manufacturer: DEK/Electro.

Photo, upper right hand corner, blue backdrop.

Verification, Ten digit cash register number above photo. Licensee's signature across middle of license.

License number, Social Security number or assigned number.

Police quick check, data is embossed. Ten digit number above picture.

I.D. card data, different from drivers license. Photo format, laminated pouch, grey data, brown and gold seals.

IDAHO

Description, photographic, polyester coating 100% plastic not laminated, black title bar. Manufacturer: DEK/Electro.

Photo, lower right hand corner, light blue background.

Verification, State Seal and director's, or commissioner's signature.

License number, Social Security or assigned numbers begining with 910 followed by six digits.

Police quick check, plastic coating on license.

I.D. card data, process and format similiar to driver's license. Marked with green bar at top, "IDAHO IDENTIFICATION CARD."

ILLINOIS

Description, photographic, laminated. manufacturer: Polaroid.

Photo, right hand side, blue backdrop.

Verification, Secretary of State's signature. Computer dot matrix printer used to print data.

License number, first letter of last name followed by 11 digits. 1st three digits = soundex code of last name. 2nd three digits = first name and middle initial coded, not sound ex. 3rd two-digits = year of birth. 4th three-digits = day and month of birth and sex coded, not Soundex.

Police quick check, State Seal, signature and three-digit number overlapping righthand edge of photo.

I.D. card data, photo and format similiar to driver's license. Marked, "ILLINOIS I.D. CARD ONLY."

INDIANA

Description, photographic, protective coating. Manufacturer: DEK/El ectro.

Photo, lower left, blue backdrop.

Verification, protective coating, concealed State Seals.

License number, Social Security number or assigned letter and nine digit number.

Police quick check, hidden State Seals.

I.D. card data, process and format, identical to driver's license. Marked on green bar, "INDIANA IDENTIFICATION CARD."

IOWA

Description, photographic, laminated. Manufacturer: Polaroid.

Photo, upper left hand corner, blue backdrop.

Verification, director's signature and station number overlap photo on right hand edge.

License number, Social Security number or assigned, nine-digit number.

Police quick check, director's signature overlaps photo.

I.D. card data, process same as driver's license. Marked "IOWA I.D". in red. Data boxes outlined in red.

KANSAS

Description, photographic, laminated. manufacturer: Polaroid.

Photo, lower right. blue backdrop.

Verification, State Seal in center of license. Two signatures overlapping edges of photo.

License number, Six alpha numerics alternating as, X4D5K6.

Police quick check, Director and Secretary of Revenue signa tures on photo edge.

I.D. card data, process same as drivers license. Marked, "KANSAS IDENTIFICATION CARD."

KENTUCKY

Description, photographic, laminated. Manufacturer:, Polaroid.

Photo, lower right, red backdrop.

Verification, State Seal. Official's signature overlaps top of photo. Camera number overlaps left hand side of photo.

License number, first letter of last name, then Soundex sys tem, 12-13 digits.

Police quick check, overlapping signature on photo. No ad dress shown for licensee.

I.D. card data, process same as drivers; license. State Seal, officials signature and camera number used. Marked "PERSONAL IDENTIFICATION".

LOUISIANA

Description, photographic, laminated, Manufacturer: DEK/Elect ro.

Photo, lower right, light blue backdrop.

Verification, State Seal on front.

License number, Nine digits, unspaced, uncoded.

Police quick check, data can be hand printed, typewritten or computer dot matrix.

I.D. card data, photo format, similiar to driver's license.

MAINE

Description, no photo, heavy paper stock, not laminated.

Photo, none.

Verification, green or black date stamp on left border of license.

License number, computer generated seven-digit number, not coded.

Police quick check, easy to alter, easy to forge. Validated with date stamp.

I.D. card data, none issued.

MARYLAND

Description, photographic, enclosed in plastic pouch. Manu facturer Polaroid.

Photo, upper left, red backdrop.

Verification, repetitive pattern of "MARYLAND" right hand side. Director's signature, back of pouch. State Seal on pouch overlapping photo.

License number, Soundex system. First letter of last name and digits 1-3 = code of last name. Digits 4-6 = code of first name. Digits 7-9 = code of middle name or initial. 10-12 = code of birth day and month.

Police quick check, State Seal on pouch overlapping photo.

I.D. card data, Two types. For non-drivers marked, "SPECIAL IDENTIFICATION CARD." For drivers marked, "AGE OF MAJORITY CARD."

MASSACHUSETTS

Description, photographic, laminated. Manufacturer: Polaroid. Gold seals on license front. Black bands sometimes appear green.

Photo, upper right, red backdrop.

Verification, Registrar's signature overlaps photo on bottom. State Seal and camera number on right hand edge of photo.

License number, Social Security number or a similiar assigned number starts with the letter "S" followed by eight digits.

Police quick check, signature and Seal overlap photo.

I.D. card data, process same as driver's license.

MICHIGAN

Description, photographic, polyester coating. Manufacturer: DEK/El ectro.

Photo, lower left, red backdrop.

Verification, large State Seal in center of license.

License number, Soundex system. First character is first letter of last (surname) name. Next three digits = code of last name. 3rd three digits = code of first name. 4th three digits = code of middle name. 5th three digits = code of month and day of birth.

Police quick check, any alteration will show breaks in lamination when viewed under special light.

I.D. card data, process same as drivers license. Different format.

MINNESOTA

Description, photographic, plastic card, like credit card. Embossed data. Manufacturer: DEK/Electro.

Photo, lower right hand corner, red backdrop.

Verification, embossed (raised) data on card.

License number, Nu-Soundex system.

Police quick check, always embossed data.

I.D. card data, process same as drivers license. Marked with green bar and "MINNESOTA IDENTIFICATION CARD."

MISSISSIPPI

Description, two types of license photo and plastic card.

Photo, full left hand side, blue backdrop.

Verification, State Seal in center of photo license.

License number, Social Security or assigned number.

Police quick check, data check only.

I.D. card data, process same as drivers's license. No special markings.

MISSOURI

Description, photographic, laminated. Manufacturer: DEK/Elect ro.

Photo, lower right hand corner, blue backdrop.

Verification, State Seal overlaps upper left hand corner of photo. Director of Revenues' signature overlaps top edge of photo, both in red.

License number, Soundex System, 16 digit number, A123-4567-12-34-5678. 1st character = first letter of last name. Next three digits = code of last name. Remainder, cod ed from, first name, middle initial, month, day of birth and sex.

Police quick check, State Seal and signature overlap top of photo.

I.D. card data, process same as drivers license. Color and format different.

MONTANA

Description, photographic, laminated transparent on front, opaque on back. Manufacturer: DEK/Electro.

Photo, lower left, blue backdrop.

Verification, State Seal center of license. Expiration in red above photo.

License number, One letter and six digits, not coded, as A 123456. First two digits = year of birth, 2nd two digits = month of birth, 3rd two digits = day of birth.

Police quick check, State Seal in gold and expiration date in red.

I.D. card data, card is blue and white, gold State Seal, color photo. Marked, "IDENTIFICATION CARD."

NEBRASKA

Description, photographic, laminated. Manufacturer: Polaroid.

Photo, lower left hand corner, red backdrop.

Verification, State Seal in center of license, director's signature overlaps photo on right hand edge.

License number, not coded. one or two letters, up to six dig its as, A02-123456.

Police quick check, blue State Seal in center of license, sig nature overlaps photo.

I.D. card data, same as drivers license. Photo format, no special markings.

NEVADA

Description, photographic, laminated both sides. Manufacturer: Polaroid.

Photo, lower right hand side, yellow backdrop.

Verification, repetitive word "Nevada" is embeded in laminate.

License number, first and last initials, year of birth, month of birth, day of birth or Social Security number.

Police quick check, director's signature overlaps top of pho- to.

I.D. card data, photographic, different from driver's license.

NEW HAMPSHIRE

Description, photographic, laminated. Manufacturer: Polaroid.

Photo, upper left hand corner, yellow backdrop.

Verification, State Seal in center of license. Director's signature overlaps photo on botton edge.

License number, number as, 03 ABC 12345. 1st two characters = month of birth. next three letters = first and last letters of last name and first letter of first name. Next four char acters = year, and day of birth. Last character used to pre vent duplication of license number.

Police quick check, license coded number against data, direct ors signature.

I.D. card data, process is same as drivers license, different format and color. Marked, "NON-DRIVER IDENTIFICATION."

NEW JERSEY

Description, two types in use: photo and non photo. Photo style laminated, Manufacturer: Polaroid. Non photo, paper stock, not laminated.

Photo, upper left hand side, red backdrop.

Verification, "New Jersey" printed in gold, across front of license. Director's signature overlaps bottom of photo.

License number, 15 alpha numeric characters, coded as, A1234 12345 12345. 1st character = first letter of last name. Next four characters = State License code. Next five characters = State license code. Last five characters = month and year of birth, eye color.

Police quick check, check for eye color, directors signature across bottom of photo.

I.D. card data, same format as drivers' license.

NEW MEXICO

Description, photographic, thin polyester coating. Manufac turer: Polaroid.

Photo, full, left hand side, red backdrop.

Verification, repeating pattern of "New Mexico" on photo.

<u>License number</u>, eight numeric digits, not coded.

<u>Police quick check</u>, "New Mexico" pattern on photo.

<u>I.D. card data</u>, process and format same as drivers' license. Red numbering.

NEW YORK

<u>Description</u>, paper stock, not laminated, no photo.

<u>Photo</u>, none.

<u>Verification</u>, data is computer dot matrix or stamped.

<u>License number</u>, 19 characters. 1st character is initial of last name. Last two digits are year of birth. Sequence = 6-5-6-2. As, A12345 12345 123456 12.

<u>Police quick check</u>, check last two digits of license number = year of birth <u>I.D. card data</u>, none issued.

NORTH CAROLINA

<u>Description</u>, photographic, laminated. Manufacturer: Polaroid.

<u>Photo</u>, upper left hand corner, red backdrop.

<u>Verification</u>, State Seal overlaps right edge of photo. Commissioner's signaturs overlaps bottom edge of photo.

<u>License number</u>, One to seven digits, no spacing, not coded.

<u>Police quick check</u>, signature and State Seal overlap photo.

<u>I.D. card data</u>, process same as drivers license. Color and format different. Marked, "SPECIAL IDENTIFICATION CARD."

NORTH DAKOTA

<u>Description</u>, photographic, laminated. Manufacturer: Polaroid.

<u>Photo</u>, full, right hand side, yellow backdrop.

<u>Verification</u>, director's signature and camera number overlap photo on left hand edge.

<u>License number</u>, Social Security or assigned number.

Police quick check, look for signature and two digit number overlapping photo on left edge.

I.D. card data, same as drivers' license. Marked, "NORTH DA KOTA IDENTIFICATION."

OHIO

Description, photographic, thin layer of polyester on front of license only. Manacturer: DEC/Electro. Data printed with computer dot matrix type.

Photo, upper right hand corner, light blue backdrop.

Verification, State Seal overlaps photo on left edge. Regist rar's signature overlaps bottom of photo.

License number, not coded, six to seven characters. First one or two characters are letters.

Police quick check, State Seal and signature overlap photo.

I.D. card data, same as drivers' license. Marked, "STATE OF OHIO IDENTIFICATION CARD".

OKLAHOMA

Description, photographic, laminated. Manufacturer: Polaroid.

Photo, upper left hand corner, blue backdrop.

Verification, Commissioner's signature overlaps photo on right edge. Camera number, three digits, on lower right hand side of license.

License number, Social Security number or assigned number up to nine digits.

Police quick check, signature overlaps photo.

I.D. card data, same as drivers' license. Marked, "OKLAHOMA IDENTIFICATION CARD" and "IDENTIFICATION NUMBER".

OREGON

Description, photographic, in plastic container. Manufac turer: Polaroid.

Photo, upper right hand corner, yellow backdrop. Backdrop co lor of photo very similar to color or license.

Verification, computer, dot matrix style printing. Administrator's signature and office number overlap photo edge.

License number, One to seven digits, not coded.

Police quick check

I.D. card data, same as drivers' license. Marked, "IDENTIFI CATION CARD".

PENNSYLVANIA

Description, Two types, photo and non-photo. Photo type, thin clear protective coating, flexible, Manufacturer: DEK/Electro. Inserts into clear plastic pouch. Non-photo type, green print on paper stock.

Photo, full, left hand side, blue backdrop.

Verification, State Seal and camera number overlaps photo on right hand edge.

License number, Eight digits, not coded.

Police quick check, State Seal and two digit number overlaps photo edge.

I.D. card data, similiar to drivers' license comes with red pouch. Marked, "IDENTIFICATION CARD." Non-photo I.D. card also available.

RHODE ISLAND

Description, photographic, laminated. Manufacturer: DEK/Elect ro.

Photo, lower right hand side, blue backdrop with black upper border.

Verification, registrar's signature on bottom of license.

License number, Seven digits, no spacing. 1st two characters are year of license issue.

Police quick check, registrar's signature.

I.D. card data, same as drivers' license. Marked in blue, "RHODE ISLAND IDENTIFICATION CARD."

SOUTH CAROLINA

Description, photographic, laminated. Manufactirer: DEK/Elect ro.

Photo, lower right hand corner, blue backdrop.

Verification, director's signature and State Seal overlaps left hand edge of photo.

License number, Five to seven numerics, not coded.

Police quick check, State Seal and signature overlaps photo.

I.D. card data, same as drivers' license. Marked with blue stripe, "RESTRICTED USE SEE REVERSE SIDE".

SOUTH DAKOTA

Description, plastic card, like credit card. Embossed data.

Photo, lower right hand corner.

Verification, data on license.

License number, 11 digits, not coded.

Police quick check, raised (embossed) data.

I.D. card data, same as drivers' license. Red stripe across top.

TENNESSEE

Description, paper stock, tamper resistant pattern printed, not laminated.

Photo, none.

Verification, Governor's and commissioner's signature on back of license.

License number, Eight digits, no spaces, not coded.

Police quick check, State Seal in yellow.

I.D. card data, Two different types issued. Marked, "FOR IDENTIFICATION PURPOSES ONLY," red lettering.

TEXAS

Description, photographic, laminated. Manufactirer: DEK/Elect ro.

Photo, full, right hand side, blue backddrop.

Verification, director's signature, State Seal across top of license.

License number, Seven or eight digits, not spaced, not coded.

Police quick check, State Seal and signature.

I.D. card data, Two different types. Marked, "FOR IDENTIFICA TION PURPOSES ONLY".

UTAH

Description, photographic, laminated. Manufacturer: DEK/Elect ro.

Photo, lower right hand corner, blue backdrop.

Verification, commissioner's signature.

License number, One letter and six digits. Letter "A" = adult, "B" = minor.

Police quick check, commissioner's signature.

I.D. card data, same as drivers license.

VERMONT

Description, Two types, paper stock or photo. Photo type is laminated.

Photo, upper left corner, dark red backdrop.

Verification, signature of commissioner on paper license. Signature overlaps photo on photo type.

License number, Eight digits, not spaced, not coded.

Police quick check, director's signature, both types.

I.D. card data, Two types, photo and non photo.

VIRGINIA

Description, Two-part license. Part A, paper stock, State seal and data portion printed with computer, dot matrix print er. Part B, photographic, plastic pouch to hold part A.

Photo, upper left hand corner, blue backdrop.

Verification, State Seal overlaps photo on part B.

License number, Social Security number or equivalent.

Police quick check, State Seal overlaps photo.

I.D. card data, same a part "B" of drivers license. Data area different.

WASHINGTON

Description, photographic, covering, polyester. Multi colored data areas. Computer dot matrix, style printing.

Photo, full right hand side, off white backdrop.

Verification, director's signature across top of photo, not overlapping.

License number, 12 characters coded as follows, first five letters of last name and initial of first name, plus middle initial. Next two characters = year of birth subtracted from 100. Remainder = special coding.

Police quick check, solid red imprint of State shape.

I.D. card data, process same as drivers' license. Marked, "WASHINGTON IDENTIFICATION CARD".

WEST VIRGINIA

Description, photographic, laminated. Manufacturer: Polaroid. State shape in blue on face of license.

Photo, upper left corner, yellow backdrop.

Verification, State Seal and camera number over lap photo on left hand edge.

License number, Seven characters, 1st digit could be letter, not coded.

Police quick check, State Seal of photo edge.

I.D. card data, process same as drivers' license, no State outline.

WISCONSIN

Description, heavy paper stock with a repeating pattern of State Seal.

Photo, no photo.

Verification, administrator's signature.

License number, Soundex system, grouped as follows: A123-1234-1234-12B. 1st letter = first letter of last name. Next three digits, = code from last name. Next three digits = code of first name and middle initial. Next two digits = year of birth. Next three digits coded from month and day of birth plus sex. Next three digits = duplication check and license type.

Police quick check, first character of license number matches first letter of last name.

I.D. card data, same as drivers license. Marked, "IDENTIFICATION CARD ONLY".

WYOMING

Description, photographic, laminated. Manufacturer: DEK/Electro. Computer, dot matrix printing for data. Cowboy riding bucking horse, outline in center of license.

Photo, lower right hand corner, light blue backdrop.

Verification, Tax Commission Chairman's signature above photo.

License number, Ten digits, no spacing, not coded.

Police quick check, computer dot matrix printing.

I.D. card data, same as drivers' license. Marked, "WYOMING IDENTIFICATION CARD ONLY".

	1. Driver Education or other Department of Education certificate meet requirements for:			2. Medical certificate required of original applicants for:				3. Driver records checked prior to issuance:			
	a. Vision	b. Knowledge and signs	c. Road test	a. Motorcycle/motorscooter	b. Bus/truck	c. Tractor-trailer	d. school bus	a. Your state	b. Prior state of residence	c. National Driver Register	d. None
UNITED STATES											
Alabama	NO	NO	NO	NO	NO	NO	NO	YES	NO	NO*	NO
Alaska	NO	NO	NO	NO	NO	NO	YES	YES	NO	YES*	NO
Arizona	NO	NO	NO	NO	NO	NO	NO	YES	YES	YES	NO
Arkansas	NO	NO	NO	NO	NO	NO	NO	NO	NO	NO	YES
California	NO	NO	NO	NO	YES	YES	YES	YES	NO	NO	NO
Colorado	NO	NO	NO	NO	NO	NO	NO	YES	NO	YES	NO
Connecticut	NO	NO	NO	NO	YES	NO	YES	YES	NO	NO	NO
Delaware	NO	YES	YES	NO	NO	NO	YES	YES	NO	NO	NO
District of Columbia	NO	NO	NO	NO*	NO*	NO*	YES	YES	NO	NO	NO
Florida	NO	NO	NO	NO	NO	NO	NO	YES	NO	NO	NO
Georgia	NO	NO	NO	NO	NO	NO	NO	YES	NO	YES	NO
Hawaii	NO	NO	NO	NO	YES*	YES*	YES	YES	NO	YES	NO
Idaho	NO	YES	YES	NO	NO	NO	NO	NO	NO	NO	YES
Illinois	NO	NO	NO	NO	NO	NO	NO*	YES	NO	NO	NO
Indiana	NO	NO	YES	NO	YES*	NO	YES	YES	YES	NO	NO
Iowa	NO	NO	YES*	NO	NO	NO	YES*	NO	NO	NO	YES*
Kansas	NO	YES	YES	NO	NO	NO	NO	NO	YES	YES	NO
Kentucky	NO	NO	NO	NO	NO	NO	NO	YES	NO	NO	NO
Louisiana	NO	NO	NO	NO	NO	NO	NO	NO	YES*	NO	NO
Maine	NO	NO	NO	NO	NO	NO	YES	YES	NO	NO	NO
Maryland	NO	NO	NO	NO	NO	NO	YES	YES	NO	YES	NO
Massachusetts	NO	NO	NO	NO	NO	NO	YES	NO	NO	NO	YES
Michigan	NO	NO	NO	NO	NO	NO	NO	YES	NO	YES	NO
Minnesota	NO	NO	NO	NO	NO	NO	YES	YES	YES	YES	NO
Mississippi	NO	NO	NO	NO	NO	NO	NO	YES	YES	YES	NO
Missouri	NO	NO	NO	NO	NO	NO	NO	YES	NO	YES	NO
Montana	NO	NO	NO	NO	NO	NO	NO*	YES	YES	YES	NO
Nebraska	NO	NO	NO	NO	YES*	YES*	YES	NO	NO	NO	YES
Nevada	NO	NO	NO	NO	YES	YES	YES	YES	YES	YES	NO
New Hampshire	NO	NO	NO	NO	NO	NO	YES	YES	NO	NO	NO
New Jersey	NO	YES	NO	NO	YES*	NO	YES*	YES	NO	YES*	YES*
New Mexico	NO	NO	NO	NO	NO	NO	YES	NO	YES	YES	NO
New York	NO	YES	NO	NO	NO	NO	NO	YES	NO	NO	NO
North Carolina	NO	NO	NO	NO	NO	NO	NO	NO	NO	NO	NO
North Dakota	NO	NO	NO	NO	NO	NO	NO	YES	NO	YES	NO
Ohio	NO	NO	NO	NO	NO	NO	YES	YES	NO	NO	NO
Oklahoma	NO	NO	NO	YES	YES	YES	NO	NO	NO	YES	NO
Oregon	NO	NO	NO	NO	NO	NO	NO	YES	NO	*	NO
Pennsylvania	NO	NO	NO	YES	YES	YES	YES	NO	NO	YES	NO
Puerto Rico	NO	NO	NO	YES	YES	YES	YES	YES	NO	NO	NO
Rhode Island	NO	NO	NO	NO	NO	NO	YES	YES	YES	YES	NO
South Carolina	NO	NO	NO	NO	NO	NO	NO	YES	YES	NO	NO
South Dakota	NO	NO	NO	NO	NO	NO	YES	YES	NO	YES*	NO
Tennessee	NO	NO	NO	NO	NO	NO	NO	YES	NO	NO	NO
Texas	NO	NO	NO	NO	NO	NO	NO*	YES	NO	YES	NO
Utah	NO	NO	NO	NO	NO	NO	NO	NO	NO	NO	YES
Vermont	NO	NO	NO	NO	NO	NO	YES*	YES	NO	YES	NO
Virginia	NO	NO	NO	NO	NO	NO	NO*	YES	NO	NO	NO
Washington	NO	NO	NO	NO	NO	NO	NO	YES*	NO	NO	NO
West Virginia	NO	NO	NO	NO*	NO*	NO*	NO*	YES	NO	NO	NO
Wisconsin	NO	NO	NO	NO	NO	NO	YES	YES	NO	YES	NO
Wyoming	NO	YES*	NO	NO*	NO*	NO*	NO*	YES	NO	YES*	NO
CANADA											
Alberta	NO	NO	NO	NO	YES	YES	YES	YES	NO	NO	NO
British Columbia	NO	NO	YES	NO	YES	YES	YES	YES	NO	NO	NO
Manitoba	NO	NO	NO	NO	YES	YES	YES	NO	NO	NO	NO
New Brunswick	NO	NO	NO	NO	YES	YES	YES	YES	NO	NO	NO
Newfoundland	NR	NR	NR	NR	NR	NR	NR	NR	NR	NR	NR
Northwest Territory	NR	NR	NR	NR	NR	NR	NR	NR	NR	NR	NR
Nova Scotia	NO	NO	NO	NO*	YES*	YES	YES	YES	YES*	NO	NO
Ontario	NO	NO	NO	NO	YES	YES	YES	YES	NO	NO	NO
Prince Edward Island	NR	NR	NR	NR	NR	NR	NR	NR	NR	NR	NR
Quebec	NO	YES	YES	NO	YES	NO	YES	YES	NO	NO	NO
Saskatchewan	NO	NO	NO	NO	YES	YES	YES	YES	YES	NO	NO
Yukon Territory	NR	NR	NR	NR	NR	NR	NR	NR	NR	NR	NR

LEGEND:
* = See text for clarification
NA = Not applicable
NR = No response
DI = Data incomplete
DNA = Data not available

	4. Type of driver license issued prior to record check: a. Temporary	b. Conditional	5. Tests required of new residents holding valid out-of-state license: Mandatory a. Vision	Mandatory b. Knowledge and signs	Mandatory c. Road test	Discretionary a. Vision	Discretionary b. Knowledge and signs	Discretionary c. Road test	6. License transmitted: a. By mail	b. In person	7. Minor and adult driver license different
UNITED STATES											
Alabama	NO	NO	YES	YES	NO	NO	NO	YES	YES	NO	NO
Alaska	NO	NO	YES	YES	NO	NO	NO	NO	NO	YES	YES
Arizona	YES	NO	YES	YES	NO	NO	NO	YES	YES	NO	NO
Arkansas	NO	NO	NO	NO	NO	NO	NO	NO	YES	NO	NO
California	YES	NO	YES	YES	NO	NO	NO	YES	YES	NO	NO
Colorado	YES	NO	YES	YES	NO	NO	NO	YES*	YES	NO	YES
Connecticut	NO	NO	YES	YES	NO	NO	NO	YES	NO	YES	NO
Delaware	NO	NO	YES	YES	NO	NO	NO	YES	NO	YES	NO
District of Columbia	NO	NO	YES	YES	NO	NO	NO	NO	NO	YES	NO
Florida	NO	NO	YES	YES	NO	NO	NO	YES	NO	YES	YES
Georgia	YES	NO	YES	YES	NO	NO	NO	NO	YES	NO	YES
Hawaii	YES	NO	YES	YES	YES	NO	NO	NO	YES	NO	YES
Idaho	NO	NO	YES	YES	NO	NO	NO	YES	YES	NO	YES
Illinois	YES	NO	YES	YES	NO	NO	NO	YES	YES	YES	NO
Indiana	NO	NO	YES	YES	YES*	NO	NO	NO	NO	YES	YES
Iowa	NO	NO	YES	YES	NO	NO	NO	YES	NO	YES*	NO
Kansas	NO	NO	YES	YES	NO	NO	NO	YES	YES	YES	NO
Kentucky	NO	NO	YES	YES	NO	NO	NO	YES	NO	YES	NO
Louisiana	NO	NO	YES	YES	NO	NO	NO	NO	YES	NO	YES
Maine	NO	NO	YES	YES	NO	NO	NO	YES	YES	YES	YES
Maryland	YES	NO	YES	YES	NO	NO	NO	YES	YES	NO	NO
Massachusetts	YES	NO	NO	NO	NO	YES	YES	YES	YES	YES	NO
Michigan	NO	NO	YES	YES	NO	NO	NO	YES	YES	NO	NO
Minnesota	YES	NO	YES	YES	YES	NO	NO	NO	YES	NO	YES
Mississippi	NO	YES	YES	YES	NO	NO	NO	YES	YES	NO	NO
Missouri	YES	NO	YES	YES	YES	NO	NO	NO	YES	NO	YES
Montana	YES	NO	YES	YES	YES	NO	NO	NO	YES	NO	NO
Nebraska	NO	NO	YES	YES	NO	NO	NO	YES	NO	YES	NO
Nevada	YES	NO	YES	YES	NO	NO	NO	YES	YES	NO	YES
New Hampshire	NO	NO	YES	YES	NO	NO	NO	YES	NO	YES	NO
New Jersey	YES	YES	YES	YES	NO	NO	NO	YES	YES	NO	NO*
New Mexico	NO	NO	YES	YES	NO	NO	NO	NO	NO	YES	YES
New York	YES	NO	YES	YES	NO	NO	NO	NO	YES	YES	YES
North Carolina	NO	NO	YES	YES	NO	NO	NO	YES	NO	YES	NO
North Dakota	YES	NO	YES	YES	NO	NO	NO	YES	YES	NO	NO
Ohio	YES	NO	YES	YES	NO	NO	NO	YES	NO	YES	YES
Oklahoma	YES	NO	YES	YES	NO	NO	NO	YES	YES*	YES*	NO
Oregon	YES	NO	YES	YES	YES*	NO	NO	YES	YES	YES	YES
Pennsylvania	NO	NO	YES	YES	NO	NO	NO	YES	YES	NO	YES
Puerto Rico	NO	NO	NO	YES	YES	NO	NO	NO	NO	YES	NO
Rhode Island	YES	NO	YES	YES	NO	NO	NO	YES	YES	NO	YES
South Carolina	YES	NO	YES	YES	NO	NO	NO	YES	YES	NO	YES
South Dakota	YES	NO	YES	YES	NO	NO	NO	YES	YES	NO	NO
Tennessee	YES	NO	YES	YES	NO	NO	NO	NO	YES	NO	NO
Texas	NO	NO	YES	YES	NO	NO	NO	YES	YES	NO	YES
Utah	YES	NO	YES	YES	NO	NO	NO	YES	YES	NO	YES
Vermont	YES	NO	YES	YES	NO	NO	NO	YES	YES	NO	YES
Virginia	YES	NO	YES	YES	NO	NO	NO	NO	YES*	YES*	NO
Washington	YES	NO	YES	YES	YES	NO	NO	NO	YES	NO	YES
West Virginia	NO	NO	NA	NA	NA	NA	NA	NA	YES	YES	YES
Wisconsin	YES	NO	YES	YES	NO	NO	NO	YES	YES	NO	NO
Wyoming	YES	NO	YES	YES	NO	NO	NO	YES	YES	NO	NO
CANADA											
Alberta	NO	NO	YES	NO	NO	NO	NO	YES	YES	YES	NO
British Columbia	YES	NO	YES	YES	NO	NO	NO	YES	YES	NO	NO
Manitoba	NO	NO	YES	NO	NO	NO	NO	NO	NO	YES	NO
New Brunswick	YES	NO	NO	NO	NO	NO	NO	NO	YES	NO	NO
Newfoundland	NR	NR	NR	NR	NR	NR	NR	NR	NR	NR	NR
Northwest Territory	NR	NR	NR	NR	NR	NR	NR	NR	NR	NR	NR
Nova Scotia	YES	NO	YES	YES*	NO	NO	NO	YES*	YES	YES	NO
Ontario	YES	NO	YES	YES	NO	NO	NO	YES	YES	NO	NO
Prince Edward Island	NR	NR	NR	NR	NR	NR	NR	NR	NR	NR	NR
Quebec	NO	NO	YES	YES	YES	NO	NO	NO	YES	NO	NO
Saskatchewan			YES	YES	NO	NO	NO	YES	YES	NO	NO
Yukon Territory	NR	NR	NR	NR	NR	NR	NR	NR	NR	NR	NR

LEGEND:
- * = See text for clarification
- NA = Not applicable
- NR = No response
- DI = Data incomplete
- DNA = Data not available

	1. Identification documents required from applicants and drivers:
UNITED STATES	
Alabama	PROPER IDENTIFICATION TO SATISFY EXAMINER
Alaska	PROPER IDENTIFICATION
Arizona	IDENTIFICATION AND SIGNATURE
Arkansas	POSITIVE IDENTIFICATION
California	SIGNATURE COMPARISON PRIOR TO ROAD TEST
Colorado	*
Connecticut	IDENTIFICATION PAPERS, CARDS, ETC.
Delaware	PRIOR LICENSE, BIRTH CERTIFICATE OR DRIVER ED. CERT.
District of Columbia	BIRTH CERTIFICATION AND SOCIAL SECURITY CARD
Florida	IDENTIFICATION REQUIRED
Georgia	SATISFACTORY EVIDENCE OF NAME AND DATE OF BIRTH
Hawaii	*
Idaho	*
Illinois	*
Indiana	REQUEST IDENTIFICATION WHEN NEEDED
Iowa	MUST SIGN THROUGHOUT THE STEPS
Kansas	BIRTH CERT., VALID LICENSE, CLEARANCE FROM STATE OF LAST ISSUANCE
Kentucky	BIRTH CERTIFICATE 16-18 YEARS OF AGE
Louisiana	AUTHENTIC DOCUMENTS SUCH AS BIRTH CERTIFICATE, PERSONAL IDENTIFICATION
Maine	BIRTH CERTIFICATE UNDER 18 YEARS OF AGE
Maryland	BIRTH CERTIFICATE, VALID DRIVERS LICENSE, SCHOOL RECORDS, OR OFFICIAL I.D. CARD
Massachusetts	BIRTH CERTIFICATE, SIGNATURE
Michigan	LEGAL IDENTIFICATION; LIST OF ACCEPTABLE DOCUMENTS IS AVAILABLE
Minnesota	*
Mississippi	POSITIVE I.D. AND SOCIAL SECURITY CARD
Missouri	IDENTIFICATION REQUIRED FROM EACH APPLICANT
Montana	BIRTH CERTIFICATE OR LICENSE
Nebraska	NONE
Nevada	REQUIRE IDENTIFICATION
New Hampshire	TWO MEANS OF IDENTIFICATION
New Jersey	BIRTH CERTIFICATE OR OTHER APPROVED IDENTIFICATION
New Mexico	BIRTH CERTIFICATE OR OTHER IDENTIFICATION
New York	PROOF OF DATE OF BIRTH AND IDENTITY
North Carolina	BIRTH CERT. OR TWO OTHER RECOGNIZED DOCUMENTS OF IDENTIFICATION
North Dakota	SATISFACTORY PROOF OF BIRTH AND SOCIAL SECURITY CARD
Ohio	BIRTH CERTIFICATE OR OTHER DOCUMENTS
Oklahoma	REQUIRED IDENTIFICATION - SIGNATURE CHECK
Oregon	DOCUMENTARY PROOF OF AGE AND TWO ADDITIONAL DOCUMENTS ESTABLISHING IDENTITY
Pennsylvania	BIRTH OR BAPTISMAL CERTIFICATE
Puerto Rico	PHOTO CHECK AGAINST LEARNER PERMIT RECORD OR OUT-OF-STATE LICENSE
Rhode Island	POSITIVE PROOF REQUIRED - HAVE PHOTO LICENSE
South Carolina	BIRTH CERTIFICATE - DOCUMENTARY EVIDENCE, ETC.
South Dakota	IF OVER 21, CURRENT LICENSE OR AFFIDAVIT; UNDER 21, BIRTH CERT. CENSUS RECORD, ETC.
Tennessee	BIRTH CERTIFICATE, OUT-OF-STATE LICENSE, ETC.
Texas	BIRTH CERTIFICATE OR OTHER ACCEPTABLE EVIDENCE OF NAME, DATE AND PLACE OF BIRTH
Utah	BIRTH CERTIFICATE OR PREVIOUSLY ISSUED DRIVER LICENSE
Vermont	REQUIRE DOCUMENTARY PROOF OF IDENTITY AND DATE AND PLACE OF BIRTH
Virginia	BIRTH CERT. OR OTHER ACCEPTABLE DOCUMENT AS PROOF OF NAME AND DOB FOR ORIGINAL
Washington	DOCUMENTS, PHOTO, AND SIGNATURE COMPARISON
West Virginia	NO RESPONSE
Wisconsin	*
Wyoming	OBSERVATION AND PERIODIC CHECKS - ALL STATIONS DO NOT HAVE INDIVIDUAL BOOTHS
CANADA	
Alberta	THREE DOCUMENTS OF IDENTIFICATION
British Columbia	*
Manitoba	LEGAL PROOF OF IDENTIFICATION, COMPARE HANDWRITING WHERE POSSIBLE
New Brunswick	SATISFACTORY PROOF OF BIRTH
Newfoundland	NO RESPONSE
Northwest Territory	NO RESPONSE
Nova Scotia	*
Ontario	PROOF OF CORRECT DATE OF BIRTH, PROVIDE PERSONAL IDENTIFICATION WITH SIGNATURE
Prince Edward Island	NO RESPONSE
Quebec	BIRTH CERTIFICATE, SOCIAL INSURANCE CARD
Saskatchewan	1 PROOF OF IDENTITY - 2 PROOF OF AGE
Yukon Territory	NO RESPONSE

LEGEND:
- * = See text for clarification
- NA = Not applicable
- NR = No response
- DI = Data incomplete
- DNA = Data not available

	2. Testing stations:			3. Method of administering knowledge and signs test:			4. Year automated test equipment put into operation:		5. Driver manual:			
	a. Number of fixed stations	b. Number of roving stations	c. Percent served by fixed stations	a. manual	b. Automated	c. Automated self administered	a. Vision	b. Knowledge and signs	a. Separate manual for each class/type of license	b. Separate sections with in manual	c. Special requirements specified in manual	d. Date last revised
UNITED STATES												
Alabama	76	0	100	YES	NO	YES	1969	1969	NO	NO	YES	1/79
Alaska	29	0	80*	YES	NO	YES	NA	1974	NA	NA	NA	7/75
Arizona	12	32	80	YES	NO	YES*	NA	1977	NO	NO	NO	5/76
Arkansas	66	0	100	YES	NO	NO	NA	NA	NO	YES	YES	6/75
California	149	58	DNA	YES	NO	NO	NA	NA	NO	YES	YES	2/79
Colorado	75	0	100	YES	NO	YES*	NA	*	YES	NO	NO	7/74
Connecticut	16	1	DNA	YES	YES	NO	NA	1979	NO	NO	NO	6/78
Delaware	4	0	100	YES	NO	NO	NA	NA	YES	NA	YES	3/76
District of Columbia	1	0	100	NO	NO	YES	NA	1974	YES	NA	YES	3/76
Florida	84	33	85	YES	NO	NO	NA	NA	NR	NR	NR	1/76
Georgia	56	98	70	YES	NO	YES	1973	1973-75	NO	YES	YES	7/79
Hawaii	19	0	100	YES	YES*	YES*	NA	1979	NO	YES	YES	10/78
Idaho	53	0	100	YES	NO	NO	NA	NA	NO	NO	YES	7/76
Illinois	123*	0	100	YES	NO	NO	NA	NA	NO	YES	YES	6/79
Indiana	187	0	100	YES	YES	NO	NA	1975	NO	YES	YES	7/76
Iowa	14	125	50	YES	NO	NO	NA	NA	NO	YES	YES	6/79
Kansas	114	0	100	YES	NO	YES	NA	1970	NO	YES	NO	5/75
Kentucky	12	108	60	YES	NO	YES	1972	1972	NA	NA	NA	1/78
Louisiana	123	0	100	YES	NO	NO	NA	NA	NO*	YES	YES	4/73
Maine	26	NR	NR	YES	NO	NO	NA	NA	NO	YES	YES	11/79
Maryland	12	5	90	YES	NO	YES	1951	1973	NO	YES	YES	6/75
Massachusetts	95	0	100	YES	NO	NO	NA	NA	YES	NO	YES	3/76
Michigan	213	0	100	YES	NO	NO	NA	NA	YES*	YES	YES	*
Minnesota	100	0	100	YES	NO	YES	NA	1974	YES	NO	YES	10/78
Mississippi	16	81	60	YES	NO	YES	NA	1973-75	NO	YES	YES	1/79
Missouri	17	120	75	YES	NO	NO	NA	NA	NO	YES	YES	12/75
Montana	58	0	100	YES	NO	NO	NA	NA	YES	YES*	YES	12/75
Nebraska	95	0	100	YES	NO	YES	NA	1973	YES	NO	YES	5/76
Nevada	8	29	88	YES	NO	YES	NA	1974	YES	NO	YES	3/76
New Hampshire	26	23	40	YES	NO	NO	NA	NA	NO	YES	YES	5/79
New Jersey	8	3	100	YES	NO	NO	NA	NA	NO*	NO	YES	1/79
New Mexico	70	0	100	YES	NO	NO	NA	NA	NO	YES	YES	3/76
New York	119	151	*	YES	NO	NO	NA	NA	YES	NO	YES	*
North Carolina	189	0	100	YES	NO	NO	NA	NA	NA*	NA	NA	1979
North Dakota	63	0	100	YES	NO	NO	NA	NA	YES	YES	YES	7/79
Ohio	93	0	100	YES	NO	NO	NA	NA	NO	YES	NO	1/76
Oklahoma	133	0	100	NO	NO	YES	1950	1971	NO	YES	YES	4/76
Oregon	57	5	98	YES	YES	YES	1979	1979	YES	NO	YES	10/79
Pennsylvania	77	0	100	YES	NO	NO	NA	NA	NA	NA	NA	7/73
Puerto Rico	9	0	100	YES	NO	NO	1975	NA	NO	NO	YES	11/74
Rhode Island	7	1*	85	YES	NO	NO	1958-59	NA	NO	NO	YES	1/72
South Carolina	67	0	100	YES	NO	NO	NA	NA	YES	NO	YES	1/75
South Dakota	3	86	50	YES	NO	NO	1959	NA	NO	NO	NO	5/75
Tennessee	12	17	NR	YES	NO	YES	NA	1972	NO	YES	NO	*
Texas	155	78	DNA	YES	NO	YES	1971	1970	NO*	YES	YES	1/79
Utah	7	6	90	YES	NO	NO	NA	NA	YES	NO	YES	2/76
Vermont	3	13	42	YES	NO	YES	NA	1972	NO	YES	YES	9/74
Virginia	35	91	80	YES	NO	YES	NA	1974	NO	YES	YES	7/76
Washington	47	5	99	YES	NO	YES	NA	1970	YES*	YES*	YES	7/79
West Virginia	59	0	100	YES	YES	NO	1971	1971	NO	NO	NO	1971
Wisconsin	25	127	80	YES	NO	NO	NA	NA	YES*	NO	YES	7/79
Wyoming	43	0	100	YES	NO	NO	1966	NA	NO	YES	YES	2/75
CANADA												
Alberta	105	0	100	YES	NO	NO	NA	NA	NO	YES	YES	7/75
British Columbia	NR	0	100	YES	NO	NO	NA	NA	YES	NO	YES	1972
Manitoba	7	11	70	YES	NO	NO	NA	NA	YES	YES	YES	6/78
New Brunswick	36	0	100	YES	NO	NO	NA	NA	NO	NO	NO	9/74
Newfoundland	NR	NR	NR	NR	NR	NR	NR	NR	NR	NR	NR	NR
Northwest Territory	NR	NR	NR	NR	NR	NR	NR	NR	NR	NR	NR	NR
Nova Scotia	57	0	100	YES	NO	NO	NA	NA	NO	YES	YES	1/75
Ontario	156	0	95	YES	NO	NO	NA	NA	NA	NA	NA	1/79*
Prince Edward Island	NR	NR	NR	NR	NR	NR	NR	NR	NR	NR	NR	NR
Quebec	50	4	95	YES	NO	NO	NA	NA	NO	NO	NO	1972
Saskatchewan	114	0	100	YES	NO	NO	NA	NA	NO	YES	YES	4/79
Yukon Territory	NR	NR	NR	NR	NR	NR	NR	NR	NR	NR	NR	NR

LEGEND:
- * = See text for clarification
- NA = Not applicable
- NR = No response
- DI = Data incomplete
- DNA = Data not available

1. Items on the individual driver's record:

	Medical record	All license applications	All examination results	Restrictions in effect	Convictions	Accident involvement	Change of license type	Change of name	DWI clinic	Driver Improvement clinic	Defense Driving course	Prior address	Advisory letters	Interviews/hearings	Suspensions	Revocations	Cancellations	Probational status	Point accumulation	Insurance information	Other
UNITED STATES																					
Alabama	YES	YES	YES	YES	YES	YES	NO	YES	NO	NO	NO	YES	NO	YES	YES	YES	YES	YES	YES	YES	NO
Alaska	NO	YES	YES	YES	YES	YES	YES	YES	YES	YES	YES	YES	YES	YES	YES	YES	YES	NO	YES	NO	NO
Arizona	YES	YES	YES	YES	YES	YES	YES	YES	YES	NO	YES	YES	YES	YES	YES	YES	YES	YES	YES	YES	NO
Arkansas	NO	NO	NO	YES	YES	YES	NO	NO	YES	NO	NO	YES	YES	YES	YES	YES	YES	YES	YES	NO	NO
California	YES	YES	YES	YES	YES	YES	YES	YES	YES	YES	YES	YES	YES	YES	YES	YES	YES	YES	YES	YES	YES*
Colorado	YES	YES	YES	YES	YES	*	YES	YES	NO	NO	NO	YES	NO	YES	YES	YES	YES	YES	YES	NO	NO
Connecticut	NO	NO	NO	NO	YES	YES	NO	YES	YES	YES	NO	NO	NO	YES	YES	YES	YES	NO	YES	NO	NO
Delaware	NO	NO	NO	NO	YES	YES	YES	YES	NO	NO	NO	YES	NO	YES	YES	YES	YES	NO	YES	YES	NO
District of Columbia	YES	YES	YES	YES	YES	YES	YES	YES	NO	NO	NO	NO	NO	YES	YES	YES	YES	YES	YES	NO	NO
Florida	NO	NO	NO	YES	YES	YES	NO	YES	YES	YES	YES	NO	NO	YES	YES	YES	YES	NO	NO	NO	NO
Georgia	YES	YES	YES	YES	YES	YES	YES	YES	YES	YES	YES	NO	NO	NO	YES	YES	YES	NO	YES	NO	NO
Hawaii *	NO	NO	NO	YES	YES	YES	NO	YES	YES	YES	NO	YES	NO	NO	YES	YES	NO	NO	YES	NO	NO
Idaho	NO	NO	NO	YES	YES	YES	YES	YES	YES	YES	YES	NO	YES	YES	YES	YES	YES	YES	YES	NO	NO
Illinois	YES	YES	YES	YES	YES	YES	YES	YES	NO	YES	NO	YES	YES	YES	YES	YES	YES	YES	YES	NO	NO
Indiana	NO	NO	NO	YES	NO	NO	YES	YES	NO	NO	YES	NO	NO	YES	YES	YES	NO	YES	YES	NO	NO
Iowa	YES	YES	YES	YES	YES	YES	YES	YES	YES	YES	NO	YES	YES	YES	YES	YES	YES	YES	NO	NO	NO
Kansas	YES	YES	NO	YES	YES	YES	YES	YES	YES	YES	NO	NO	NO	NO	YES	YES	YES	YES	NO	NO	NO
Kentucky	NO	NO	NO	YES	YES	YES	YES	YES	YES	YES	NO	NO	YES	YES	YES	YES	YES	YES	YES	NO	NO
Louisiana	NO	NO	NO	YES	YES	YES	NO	NO	NO	NO	NO	NO	NO	YES	YES	YES	YES	NO	NO	YES	YES*
Maine	YES	YES*	NO	YES	YES	YES	YES	YES	YES	YES	NO	YES	NO	YES	YES	YES	YES	YES	YES	YES	NO
Maryland	NO	YES	NO	YES	YES	YES	YES	YES	NO	YES	NO	NO	YES	YES	YES	YES	YES	NO	YES	NO	NO
Massachusetts	YES	NO	NO	YES	YES	NO	YES	YES	YES	YES	NO	YES	YES	YES	YES	YES	YES	YES	NO	NO	NO
Michigan	YES	NO	NO	YES	YES	YES	YES	YES	YES	YES	NO	YES	YES	YES	YES	YES	YES	YES	YES	NO	NO
Minnesota	YES	NO	NO	YES	YES	YES	NO	YES	YES	YES	NO	NO	YES	YES	YES	YES	YES	NO	NO	NO	NO
Mississippi	YES	YES	YES	YES	YES	YES	YES	YES	YES	NO	NO	NO	YES	YES	YES	YES	YES	YES	NO	NO	NO
Missouri	NO	NO	NO	YES	YES	NO	NO	NO	NO	NO	NO	NO	NO	NO	YES	YES	NO	NO	YES	NO	NO
Montana	YES	YES	YES	YES	YES	YES	YES	YES	NO	NO	NO	YES	NO	YES	YES	YES	YES	YES	YES	NO	NO
Nebraska	YES	YES	YES	YES	YES	YES	YES	YES	NO	NO	NO	NO	YES	NO	YES	YES	YES	YES	YES	NO	NO
Nevada	NO	NO	NO	YES	NO	NO	NO	NO	NO	NO	NO	NO	NO	NO	YES	YES	YES	NO	YES	NO	YES*
New Hampshire	YES	NO	NO	YES	YES	YES	NO	YES	YES	YES	NO	YES	YES	YES	YES	YES	NO	YES	NO	YES	YES*
New Jersey	NO	NO	NO	YES	YES	YES	NO	YES	NO	YES	NO	NO	YES	NO	YES	YES	NO	NO	YES	NO	NO
New Mexico	NO	YES	NO	YES	YES	YES	NO	NO	YES	NO	NO	NO	YES	NO	YES	YES	YES	YES	YES	NO	NO
New York	YES*	NO	NO	YES	YES	YES	YES	YES	YES	YES	YES	NO	YES	YES	YES	YES	YES	YES	YES	NO	NO
North Carolina	YES	YES	NO	YES	YES	YES	YES	YES	NO	YES	NO	YES	YES	YES	YES	YES	YES	YES	YES	NO	YES*
North Dakota	NO	NO	YES	YES	YES	YES	YES	NO	NO	NO	YES	NO	NO	NO	YES	YES	YES	NO	YES	YES	NO
Ohio	YES	NO	NO	YES	YES	YES	YES	YES	NO	YES	YES	NO	YES	NO	YES	YES	NO	YES	YES	NO	NO
Oklahoma	YES	NO	NO	YES	YES	YES	YES	YES	NO	NO	NO	NO	YES	YES	YES	YES	YES	NO	NO	NO	NO
Oregon	YES	NO	YES	YES	YES	YES	NO	NO	YES	YES	YES	NO	YES	YES	YES	YES	YES	YES	NO	YES	NO
Pennsylvania	NO	NO	NO	YES	YES	YES	NO	YES	NO	YES	NO	NO	YES	YES	YES	YES	NO	NO	YES	NO	NO
Puerto Rico	YES	YES	YES	YES	YES	NO	YES	YES	YES	YES	YES	YES	YES	YES	YES	YES	YES	YES	YES	NO	NO
Rhode Island	YES	YES	NO	YES	YES	YES	NO	YES	YES	NA	NA	YES	YES	YES	YES	YES	YES	YES	NA	NA	NO
South Carolina	NO	NO	NO	YES	YES	YES	NO	YES	NO	NO	YES	YES	YES	NO	YES	YES	YES	YES	YES	YES	NO
South Dakota	YES	NO	YES	YES	YES	YES	YES	NO	NO	NO	NO	NO	YES	YES	YES	YES	YES	YES	NO*	NO	NO
Tennessee	NO	NO	NO	YES	YES	YES	YES	YES	YES	YES	NO	NO	YES	YES	YES	YES	YES	YES	NO	NO	NO
Texas	NO	YES	NO	YES	YES	YES	YES	YES	YES	YES	YES	NO	NO	YES	YES	NO	YES	YES	NO	NO	NO
Utah	YES	YES	YES	YES	YES*	YES	YES	YES	YES	YES	YES	YES	NO	YES	YES	YES	YES	YES	YES	YES	NO
Vermont	NO	YES	NO	YES	YES	YES	YES	YES	NO	NO	NO	NO	YES	NO	YES	YES	NO	NO	NO	YES	NO
Virginia	YES	YES	YES	YES	YES	YES	YES	YES	YES	YES	YES	YES	YES	YES	YES	YES	YES	YES	YES	YES	YES*
Washington	YES	YES	YES	YES	YES	NO	YES	YES	NO	YES	NO	NO	YES	YES	YES	YES	YES	YES	YES	NO	NO
West Virginia	NO	NO	NO	YES	YES	YES	YES	YES	NO	NO	YES	NO	YES	YES	YES	YES	NO	YES	YES	NO	NO
Wisconsin	YES	YES	NO	YES	YES	YES	YES	YES	YES	YES	NO	NO	YES	YES	YES	YES	YES	YES	YES	NO	NO
Wyoming	YES	NO	YES	YES	YES	YES	YES	YES	NO	NO	YES	NO	YES	YES	YES	YES	YES	NO	NO	YES	NO
CANADA																					
Alberta	YES	NO	YES	YES	YES	YES	YES	YES	YES	YES	YES	YES	YES	NO	YES	NO	YES	YES	YES	NO	NO
British Columbia	YES*	YES*	YES*	YES	YES	YES	NO	NO	NO	NO	YES	NO	YES	NO	YES	NO	NO	NO	YES	NO	YES*
Manitoba	YES	NO	NO	YES	YES	YES	YES	YES	YES	YES	YES	NO	YES	YES	YES	YES	YES	YES	YES	YES	NO
New Brunswick	NO	NO	NO	NO	YES	YES	NO	NO	NO	YES	NO	NO	YES	YES	YES	YES	NO	YES	YES	YES	NO
Newfoundland	NR	NR	NR	NR	NR	NR	NR	NR	NR	NR	NR	NR	NR	NR	NR	NR	NR	NR	NR	NR	NR
Northwest Territory	NR	NR	NR	NR	NR	NR	NR	NR	NR	NR	NR	NR	NR	NR	NR	NR	NR	NR	NR	NR	NR
Nova Scotia	YES	NO	YES	YES	YES	YES	NO	YES	YES	YES	YES	YES	YES	YES	YES	YES	YES	YES	YES	YES*	NO
Ontario	YES	YES	YES	YES	YES	YES	YES	YES	NO	YES	NO	YES	YES	YES	YES	YES	YES	NO	YES	NO	NO
Prince Edward Island	NR	NR	NR	NR	NR	NR	NR	NR	NR	NR	NR	NR	NR	NR	NR	NR	NR	NR	NR	NR	NR
Quebec	YES*	YES	YES	YES	YES	NO	YES	YES	NO	NO	NO	YES	NO	NO	YES	YES	YES	NO	YES	NO	NO
Saskatchewan	YES	NO	NO	YES	YES	NO	YES	NO	NO	YES	NO	NO	YES	YES	YES	YES	NO	NO	YES	NO	NO
Yukon Territory	NR	NR	NR	NR	NR	NR	NR	NR	NR	NR	NR	NR	NR	NR	NR	NR	NR	NR	NR	NR	NR

LEGEND:
- * = See text for clarification
- NA = Not applicable
- NR = No response
- DI = Data incomplete
- DNA = Data not available

	2. Agency primarily responsible for the operation and maintenance of the main frame:
UNITED STATES	
Alabama	DEPT. OF PUBLIC SAFETY
Alaska	DEPT. OF PUBLIC SAFETY
Arizona	RECORDS SECTION
Arkansas	NOT AUTOMATED
California	DMV, DIVISION OF EDP SERVICES
Colorado	NO RESPONSE
Connecticut	ADMINISTRATIVE SERVICES
Delaware	DEPT. OF PUBLIC SAFETY
District of Columbia	D.C. GOVT., BUREAU OF MOTOR VEHICLES
Florida	DEPT. OF HWY. SAFETY AND MOTOR VEHICLES
Georgia	DEPT. OF ADMINISTRATIVE SERVICES
Hawaii	STATE TRAFFIC VIOLATIONS BUREAU
Idaho	DEPT. OF TRANSPORTATION
Illinois	DATA PROCESSING DEPT., OFFICE OF SECRETARY OF STATE
Indiana	BUREAU OF MOTOR VEHICLES
Iowa	DRIVERS LICENSE, DEPT. OF TRANSPORTATION
Kansas	DRIVERS LICENSE SECTION
Kentucky	DEPT. OF JUSTICE, BUREAU OF STATE POLICE; DEPT. OF TRANSPORTATION, DIVISION OF DRIVER LICENSING
Louisiana	DRIVERS LICENSE BUREAU
Maine	CENTRAL COMPUTER SERVICES, BUREAU OF FINANCE AND ADMINISTRATION
Maryland	DEPT. OF TRANSPORTATION
Massachusetts	REGISTRY OF MOTOR VEHICLES
Michigan	BUREAU OF REGULATORY AND LICENSING DATA CENTER, DRIVER AND VEHICLE ADMINSTRATION
Minnesota	LICENSING AND RECORDS, DRIVER AND VEHICLE SERVICES DIVISION
Mississippi	CENTRAL DATA PROCESSING AUTHORITY
Missouri	INFORMATION SYSTEMS DIVISION
Montana	MONTANA HIGHWAY DEPT.
Nebraska	CENTRAL DATA PROCESSING
Nevada	STATE COMPUTER FACILITY
New Hampshire	FINANCIAL RESPONSIBILITY SECTION, DEPT. OF MOTOR VEHICLES
New Jersey	DIVISION OF SYSTEMS AND COMMUNICATIONS
New Mexico	NO RESPONSE
New York	OFFICE OF DATA PROCESSING
North Carolina	SOFTWARE-N.C. DOT; HARDWARE - IBM
North Dakota	DRIVERS LICENSE DIVISION; STATE HIGHWAY DEPT.
Ohio	DEPT. OF HIGHWAY SAFETY
Oklahoma	CENTRAL FILES
Oregon	MOTOR VEHICLES DIVISION
Pennsylvania	BUREAU OF MANAGEMENT INFORMATION SERVICES
Puerto Rico	DEPT. OF TRANSPORTATION AND PUBLIC WORKS
Rhode Island	REGISTRY OF MOTOR VEHICLES
South Carolina	NO RESPONSE
South Dakota	DRIVER LICENSE ISSUANCE
Tennessee	DEPT. OF SAFETY
Texas	DEPT. OF PUBLIC SAFETY
Utah	STATE INFORMATION SYSTEMS CENTER
Vermont	STATE INFORMATION SYSTEM
Virginia	DIVISION OF AUTOMATED DATA PROCESSING
Washington	DEPT. OF MOTOR VEHICLES
West Virginia	DEPT. OF FINANCE AND ADMIN., ISSD DIVISION AND IBM FOR MAINTENANCE
Wisconsin	DIV. OF BUREAU MANAGEMENT D.O.T.
Wyoming	DEPT. OF REVENUE AND TAXATION, MOTOR VEHICLE DIVISION
CANADA	
Alberta	CENTRAL DATA CENTER
British Columbia	COMPUTER AND CONSULTING SERVICES BRANCH
Manitoba	MANITOBA DATA SERVICES
New Brunswick	MOTOR VEHICLE BRANCH - DRIVER RECORDS
Newfoundland	NO RESPONSE
Northwest Territory	NO RESPONSE
Nova Scotia	NOT AUTOMATED
Ontario	GOVERNMENT SERVICES
Prince Edward Island	NO RESPONSE
Quebec	BUREAU DES VEHICULES AUTOMOBILES
Saskatchewan	HIGHWAY TRAFFIC BOARD
Yukon Territory	NO RESPONSE

LEGEND:
- * = See text for clarification
- NA = Not applicable
- NR = No response
- DI = Data incomplete
- DNA = Data not available

	3. Driver status available to all law forcement agencies on a 24-hour, 7-day	4. Automated driver records filed: a. Alphabetic	b. Alpha-numeric	c. Numeric	d. Other	5. System automatically identifies: a. Habitual offenders	b. Problem Drivers	c. Drivers eligible for and referred to Driver Improvement program	d. Suspensions and revocations	e. Any subset	6. Minimum period (in years) for retention of a complete driver's record:
UNITED STATES											
Alabama	NO	NO	YES	NO	YES*	NO	NO	NO	YES	NO	7
Alaska	YES	YES	NO	YES	NO	YES	YES	YES	YES	NO	3
Arizona	YES	YES	YES	YES	YES*	YES	YES	NO	YES	NO	5
Arkansas	YES	NO	NO	NO	YES*	NO	NO	NO	NO	NO	3
California	YES	NO	YES	NO	NO	YES	YES	YES	YES	YES	8
Colorado	YES	NO	NO	YES	YES*	YES	YES	YES	YES	NO	3
Connecticut	NO	NO	YES	NO	NO	YES	YES	YES	YES	NO	5
Delaware	YES	NR	NR	NR	NR	YES	YES	YES	YES	NO	*
District of Columbia	NO	NO	YES	NO	NO	NO	NO	YES	YES	NO	7
Florida	YES	NO	YES	NO	NO	YES	NO	NO	YES	NO	5
Georgia	YES	YES	YES	YES	NO	YES	YES	NO	YES	NO	10
Hawaii	YES	YES	NO	YES	NO	NO	NO	NO	YES	NO	7
Idaho	YES	YES	NO	YES	NO	YES	YES	YES	YES	NO	5
Illinois	YES	NO	YES	NO	NO	NO	NO	YES	YES	NO	4
Indiana	YES	NO	YES	NO	YES*	YES	NO	YES	NO	NO	10
Iowa	YES	YES	YES	NO	NO	YES	YES	YES	YES	NO	5
Kansas	YES	YES	NO	NO	NO	YES	NO	YES	YES	YES*	*
Kentucky	YES	NO	YES	NO	NO	YES	YES	YES	YES	NO	5
Louisiana	YES	YES	NO	YES	NO	YES	YES	YES	YES	NO	1
Maine	YES	NO	NO	NO	YES*	YES	YES	NO	YES	NO	5
Maryland	YES	YES	YES*	NO	NO	YES	YES	YES	YES	NO	3
Massachusetts	YES	YES	YES	NO	YES*	YES	YES	YES	YES	YES	*
Michigan	YES	NO	YES	NO	NO	YES	YES	YES	YES	YES	7
Minnesota	YES	NO	YES	NO	NO	NO	NO	NO	YES	NO	5
Mississippi	YES	YES	YES	YES	NO	NO	YES	NO	YES	NO	3*
Missouri	YES	YES	YES	NO	NO	YES	NO	NO	YES	NO	NR
Montana	YES	YES	NO	NO	NO	NA*	NA*	NA*	NA*	NA*	5
Nebraska	YES	YES	YES	NO	YES*	NR	NR	NR	NR	NR	1
Nevada	YES	NO	YES	NO	NO	NO	NO	NO	YES	NO	4
New Hampshire	YES	YES	NO	NO	NO	YES*	YES*	NO	YES*	NO	7*
New Jersey	YES	YES	YES	YES	NO	YES	YES	YES	YES	NO	3
New Mexico	YES	YES	NO	NO	NO	YES	YES	YES	YES	YES	2½
New York	YES	NO	YES	NO	NO	YES	YES	YES	YES	NO	4
North Carolina	YES	YES	NO	YES	YES*	YES	YES	YES	YES	NO	5
North Dakota	YES	YES	NO	YES	NO	YES	NO	NO	YES	NO	3
Ohio	YES	YES	YES	NO	NO	YES	YES	NO	YES	NO	*
Oklahoma	YES	YES	YES	YES	NO	NO	NO	YES	YES	NO	5
Oregon	YES	YES	NO	YES	NO	YES	YES	YES	YES	NO	10
Pennsylvania	YES	NO	YES*	NO	NO	NO	NO	YES	YES	NO	3
Puerto Rico	YES	NO	NO	YES	NO	NO	NO	YES	YES	NO	*
Rhode Island	NO*	NO	NO	YES	YES*	NO	NO	NO	NO	NO	3
South Carolina	YES	NO	NO	YES	NO	YES	NO	NO	YES	NO	10
South Dakota	NO	NO	NO	YES	NO	NA	NA	NA	NA	NA	4
Tennessee	YES	YES	YES	YES	NO	YES	YES	YES	YES	NO	5
Texas	YES	YES	NO	YES	NO	YES	YES	YES	YES	NO	*
Utah	YES	NO	NO	NO	YES*	YES	YES	YES	YES	NO	NR
Vermont	YES	NO	YES	NO	NO	YES	YES	NO	YES	NO	8
Virginia	YES	NO	YES	NO	NO	YES	YES	YES	YES	NO	8
Washington	YES	NO	YES	NO	NO	YES	YES	YES	YES	NO	5
West Virginia	YES	NR	NR	NR	NR	NO	YES	YES	YES	NO	7
Wisconsin	YES	NO	YES	NO	NO	NO	YES	YES	YES	NO	4
Wyoming	YES	YES	NO	NO	NO	NO	NO	NO	NO	YES	3
CANADA											
Alberta	NO	YES	NO	YES	NO	YES	YES	YES	YES	NO	NA
British Columbia	YES	NO	NO	YES	NO	YES*	YES*	YES*	NO	NO	5
Manitoba	YES	NO	YES	NO	NO	NO	NO	YES	YES	NO	5
New Brunswick	NO	NO	YES*	NO	NO	YES	YES	YES	YES	NO	5
Newfoundland	NR	NR	NR	NR	NR	NR	NR	NR	NR	NR	NR
Northwest Territory	NR	NR	NR	NR	NR	NR	NR	NR	NR	NR	NR
Nova Scotia	NO	YES*	YES*	NO	NO	YES*	YES*	YES*	YES*	NO	5
Ontario	NO	NO	YES	NO	NO	YES	YES	YES	YES	NO	6*
Prince Edward Island	NR	NR	NR	NR	NR	NR	NR	NR	NR	NR	NR
Quebec	YES	NO	YES	NO	NO	YES	NO	NO	YES	NO	3
Saskatchewan	NO	YES	NO	NO	NO	NO	NO	NO	NO	NO	5
Yukon Territory	NR	NR	NR	NR	NR	NR	NR	NR	NR	NR	NR

LEGEND:

- * = See text for clarification
- NA = Not applicable
- NR = No response
- DI = Data incomplete
- DNA = Data not available

	7. Driver records updated: a. Daily	b. Weekly	c. Other	8. Driver records purged: a. Daily	b. Weekly	c. Other	9. Criteria for purging driver record files: a. Vital statistics	b. Driver license returned by another state	c. Voluntary surrender of driver license	d. Other	10. Maintain file of all purged driver records for statistical purposes:
UNITED STATES											
Alabama	YES	NO	NO	YES	NO	NO	NO	YES	YES	YES*	NO
Alaska	NO	YES	NO	*	*	*	*	*	*	*	NA
Arizona	YES	NO	NO	NO	NO	YES*	YES	YES	YES	NO	YES
Arkansas	YES	NO	NO	NO	NO	YES*	YES	NO	NO	NO	YES
California	YES	NO	NO	NO	YES	NO	NO	NO	NO	YES*	NO
Colorado	YES	NO	NO	YES	NO	NO	NO	NO	NO	YES*	YES
Connecticut	NO	YES	NO	NO	NO	YES*	NO	NO	NO	YES*	NO
Delaware	YES	NO	NO	NO	NO	YES*	NO	YES	YES	NO	YES
District of Columbia	YES	NO	NO	YES	NO	NO	NO	YES	YES	NO	YES
Florida	NO	YES	NO	NO	YES	NO	YES	NO	YES	YES*	YES
Georgia	NO	NO	YES*	NO	NO	YES*	NO	YES	YES	YES*	YES
Hawaii	YES	NO	NO	YES	NO	NO	NO	NO	NO	YES*	YES
Idaho	YES	NO	NO	NO	NO	YES*	YES	YES	YES	YES*	YES
Illinois	YES	NO	NO	NO	NO	YES*	YES	NO	NO	YES*	YES
Indiana	NO	YES	NO	NO	NO	YES*	NO	NO	NO	YES*	NO
Iowa	YES	NO	NO	YES	NO	YES*	YES	NO	NO	YES*	NO
Kansas	YES	NO	NO	NO	NO	YES*	YES	YES	YES	YES*	YES
Kentucky	YES	NO	NO	YES	NO	NO	NO	NO	NO	YES*	NO
Louisiana	YES	NO	NO	NR	NR	NR	YES	YES	YES	YES*	NO
Maine	YES	NO	NO	NO	NO	YES*	NO	NO	NO	YES*	YES
Maryland	YES	NO	NO	YES	NO	NO	NO	NO	NO	YES*	YES
Massachusetts	YES	NO	NO	NO	NO	YES*	NO	NO	NO	YES*	YES
Michigan	YES*	YES*	NO	NO	NO	YES*	NO	NO	NO	YES*	NO
Minnesota	YES	NO	YES*	NO	NO	YES*	NO	NO	NO	YES*	NO
Mississippi	YES	YES	NO	NO	YES	NO	YES	YES	YES	NO	NO
Missouri	YES	NO	NO	NO	NO	YES*	YES	NO	NO	YES*	YES
Montana	NO	YES	NO	NA*	NA*	NA*	NA*	NA*	NA*	NA*	NA*
Nebraska	YES	NO	NO	NO	NO	YES*	NO	NO	NO	YES*	NO
Nevada	YES	NO	NO	YES	NO	NO	YES	NO	NO	YES*	NA
New Hampshire	NR	NR	NR	NO	NO	YES*	YES	YES	YES	YES*	NO
New Jersey	NO	YES	NO	NO	NO	YES*	NO	NO	NO	YES*	YES
New Mexico	NO	YES	NO	NO	NO	YES*	NO	YES	YES	YES*	NO
New York	YES	NO	NO	NO	NO	YES*	NO	NO	NO	YES*	NO
North Carolina	YES	NO	NO	NO	NO	YES*	NO	NO	NO	YES*	YES
North Dakota	YES	NO	NO	NO	NO	YES*	NO	NO	NO	YES*	NO
Ohio	YES	NO	NO	NO	NO	YES*	NO	NO	NO	YES*	YES
Oklahoma	YES	NO	NO	NO	NO	YES*	NO	NO	NO	YES*	NO
Oregon	YES	NO	NO	NO	NO	YES*	NO	NO	NO	YES*	YES
Pennsylvania	YES	NO	NO	NO	NO	YES*	YES	NO	NO	YES*	NO
Puerto Rico	YES	NO	NO	YES	NO	NO	NO	YES	YES	YES*	YES
Rhode Island	YES	NO	NO	NO	NO	YES*	NR	NR	NR	NR	NO
South Carolina	YES	NO	NO	NR	NR	NR	NO	YES	YES	YES*	YES
South Dakota	YES	NO	NO	NO	NO	YES*	YES	YES	NO	NO	NO
Tennessee	YES	NO	NO	NO	NO	YES*	NO	YES	NO	YES*	YES
Texas	YES	NO	NO	NO	YES	NO	NO	NO	NO	YES*	NO
Utah	YES	NO	NO	NO	NO	YES*	NO	NO	NO	YES*	YES
Vermont	YES	NO	NO	NO	NO	YES*	NO	NO	YES	YES*	YES
Virginia	NO	NO	YES*	NO	NO	YES*	NO	NO	NO	YES*	YES
Washington	YES*	YES*	NO	NO	NO	YES*	YES	NO	NO	YES*	YES
West Virginia	YES	NO	NO	NO	NO	YES*	NR	NR	NR	NR	YES
Wisconsin	YES	NO	NO	NO	NO	YES*	NO	NO	NO	YES*	NO
Wyoming	YES	NO	NO	NO	NO	YES*	YES	YES	YES	NO	YES
CANADA											
Alberta	NO	YES	NO	NO	YES	NO	YES	YES	YES	NO	NA
British Columbia	NO	YES	NO	NO	NO	YES*	YES	NO	NO	NO	YES
Manitoba	NO	NO	YES*	NO	NO	YES*	NO	YES	NO	YES*	NO
New Brunswick	YES	NO	NO	NO	NO	YES*	NO	NO	NO	YES*	NO*
Newfoundland	NR	NR	NR	NR	NR	NR	NR	NR	NR	NR	NR
Northwest Territory	NR	NR	NR	NR	NR	NR	NR	NR	NR	NR	NR
Nova Scotia	NO	NO	YES*	NO	NO	YES*	NO	NO	NO	YES*	NO
Ontario	YES	NO	NO	NO	NO	YES*	NO	NO	NO	YES*	YES
Prince Edward Island	NR	NR	NR	NR	NR	NR	NR	NR	NR	NR	NR
Quebec	YES	NO	NO	NO	YES	NO	NO	YES	YES	YES*	YES
Saskatchewan	YES	NO	NO	NO	NO	NO	NA	NA	NA	NA	NA
Yukon Territory	NR	NR	NR	NR	NR	NR	NR	NR	NR	NR	NR

LEGEND:
- * = See text for clarification
- NA = Not applicable
- NR = No response
- DI = Data incomplete
- DNA = Data not available

	23. Use the National Driver Register:	24. In calendar 1978 the number of :			25. Use Uniform Traffic Ticket and Complaint				26. State level control and audit of all tickets issued to law enforcement agencies	27. All out-of-state convictions treated as though occurred in-state
		a. Queries	b. Positives (showing suspension, revocation or cancellation)	c. Additions		a. at state level	b. at county level	c. at local level		
UNITED STATES										
Alabama	YES	120,000	3,322	64,499	YES	YES	YES	YES	YES	NO*
Alaska	YES	49,000	2,450	5,000	NR	NR	NR	NR	NR	NR
Arizona	YES	26,670*	765*	386*	YES	YES	YES	YES	YES	YES
Arkansas	DNA	DNA	DNA	DNA	NR	NR	NR	NR	NR	NR
California	YES	DNA	DNA	197,000	NO	NA	NA	NA	NO	NO*
Colorado	YES	100,000	DNA	DNA	NR	NR	NR	NR	NR	NR
Connecticut	YES	NR	NR	NR	NR	NR	NR	NR	NR	NR
Delaware	YES	DNA	DNA	DNA	YES	YES	YES	YES	YES	YES
District of Columbia	YES	DNA	DNA	DNA	NR	NR	NR	NR	NR	NR
Florida	NO	NA	NA	NA	YES	YES	YES	YES	YES	YES*
Georgia	YES	DNA	DNA	DNA	YES	YES	YES	YES	NO	YES
Hawaii	YES	115,000	1,000	50	YES	YES	YES	NA	YES	NO*
Idaho	YES	3,861	186	3,282	NR	NR	NR	NR	NR	NR
Illinois	YES	DNA	NR	11,855	YES	YES	YES	YES*	NO	YES
Indiana	YES	DNA	DNA	DNA	NR	NR	NR	NR	NR	NR
Iowa	YES	600,000	1,000	DNA	YES	YES	YES	YES	*	YES
Kansas	YES	DNA	DNA	DNA	NR	NR	NR	NR	NR	NR
Kentucky	YES	*	DNA	7,200	YES	YES	NO	NO	YES	NO*
Louisiana	YES	140,000	5,188	26,000	NR	NR	NR	NR	NR	NR
Maine	YES	NR	NR	NR	YES	YES	YES	YES	YES	YES
Maryland	YES	*	4,000	195,000	YES	YES	YES	YES	YES	NO*
Massachusetts	YES	90,000	9,000	DI	NR	NR	NR	NR	NR	NR
Michigan	YES	1,000,000	NR	NR	NR	NR	NR	NR	NR	NR
Minnesota	YES	DNA	DNA	19,548	YES	YES	YES	YES	NO	YES
Mississippi	YES	NR	NR	NR	NO	NA	NA	NA	YES*	YES
Missouri	YES	*	NA	NA	NR	NR	NR	NR	NR	NR
Montana	YES	DNA	DNA	5,377	NR	NR	NR	NR	NR	NR
Nebraska	NO	NA	NA	NA	YES	YES	YES	YES	NO	NO*
Nevada	YES	*	6,569	1,028	*	NA	NA	NA	NA	NA
New Hampshire	YES	DI	DNA	DI	NR	NR	NR	NR	NR	NR
New Jersey	YES	DNA	DNA	DNA	YES	YES	YES	YES	YES	NO*
New Mexico	YES	NR	NR	NR	NR	NR	NR	NR	NR	NR
New York	YES	*	DNA	*	YES	YES	YES	YES	YES	NO*
North Carolina	YES	DNA	DNA	DNA	YES	YES	YES	YES	YES	NO*
North Dakota	YES	170,000	1,000	170,000	YES	YES	YES	NO	*	NO*
Ohio	YES	643,913	6,200	42,141	NR	NR	NR	NR	NR	NR
Oklahoma	YES	DNA	DNA	NR	NR	NR	NR	NR	NR	NR
Oregon	YES	100,000	DNA	DNA	YES	YES	YES	YES	NO	YES
Pennsylvania	YES	360,000	DNA	10,650	YES	YES	YES	YES*	YES	NO
Puerto Rico	NR	NR	NR	NR	NO	NA	NA	NA	NO	NR
Rhode Island	YES	DI	DI	DI	NR	NR	NR	NR	NR	NR
South Carolina	YES	NR	DNA	22,272	YES	YES	YES	YES	YES	NO*
South Dakota	YES	220	120	60,000	YES	YES	YES	YES	NO	YES
Tennessee	YES	NA	NA	NA	NR	NR	NR	NR	NR	NR
Texas	YES	*	DNA	57,663	NO	NA	NA	NA	NO	NO*
Utah	YES	250	DNA	10,855	NR	NR	NR	NR	NR	NR
Vermont	YES	DNA	DNA	DNA	NR	NR	NR	NR	NR	NR
Virginia	YES	297,157	6,230	30,379	NR	NR	NR	NR	NR	NR
Washington	YES	DNA	DNA	DNA	YES	YES	YES	YES	YES	YES
West Virginia	YES	NR	NR	NR	NR	NR	NR	NR	NR	NR
Wisconsin	YES	*	NR	30,348	YES	YES	YES	YES	YES	NO*
Wyoming	YES	DI	259	NA	NR	NR	NR	NR	NR	NR
CANADA										
Alberta	NO	NA	NA	NA	NR	NR	NR	NR	NR	NR
British Columbia	NO	NA	NA	NA	YES	YES	NO	NO	YES	NO*
Manitoba	NO	NA	NA	NA	YES	YES	YES	YES	NO	YES
New Brunswick	NO	NA	NA	NA	NO	NA	NA	NA	YES	NO
Newfoundland	NR	NR	NR	NR	NR	NR	NR	NR	NR	NR
Northwest Territory	NR	NR	NR	NR	NR	NR	NR	NR	NR	NR
Nova Scotia	NO	NA	NA	NA	YES	YES	YES	YES	YES	YES
Ontario	NO	NA	NA	NA	NR	NR	NR	NR	NR	NR
Prince Edward Island	NR	NR	NR	NR	NR	NR	NR	NR	NR	NR
Quebec	NO	NA	NA	NA	NO	NA	NA	NA	NO	YES*
Saskatchewan	NO	NA	NA	NA	NR	NR	NR	NR	NR	NR
Yukon Territory	NR	NR	NR	NR	NR	NR	NR	NR	NR	NR

LEGEND:
- * = See text for clarification
- NA = Not applicable
- NR = No response
- DI = Data incomplete
- DNA = Data not available

	28. Receive notification from other states when they suspend or revoke driving priviledge of your drivers:	a. From all states	b. Number of states	29. Notify home state when you suspend or revoke the driving priviledge of an out-of-state driver:	a. All states	b. Number of states	30. Receive certificates of conviction from other states of your convicted state drivers:	a. From all states	b. Number of states	1. Forward certificates of conviction to home state of convicted out-of-state drivers:	a. All states	b. Number of states
UNITED STATES												
Alabama	YES	NO	MOST	YES	YES	NA	YES	NO	MOST	YES	YES	NA
Alaska	YES	YES	NA	YES	YES	NA	YES	YES	NA	YES	YES	NA
Arizona	YES	NO	*	YES	YES	NA	YES	YES	NA	YES	YES	NA
Arkansas	YES	YES	NA	YES	YES	NA	YES	YES	NA	YES	YES	NA
California	YES	YES	NA	YES	YES	NA	YES	YES	NA	YES	YES	NA
Colorado	YES	YES	NA	YES	YES	NA	YES	YES	NA	YES	YES	NA
Connecticut	YES	NO	DNA	NR	NR	NR	NR	NR	NR	NR	NR	NR
Delaware	YES	YES*	47*	YES	YES*	47*	YES	YES*	47*	YES	YES*	47*
District of Columbia	YES	NO	MOST	YES	YES	NA	YES	NO	MOST	YES	YES	NA
Florida	YES	YES*	NA	YES	YES	NA	YES	YES*	NA	YES	YES	NA
Georgia	YES	NO	MOST	NO	NA	NA	YES	NO	MOST	NO	NA	NA
Hawaii	YES	YES	NA	YES	YES	NA	YES	YES	NA	NO	NA	NA
Idaho	YES	YES	NA	YES	YES	NA	YES	YES	NA	YES	YES	NA
Illinois	YES	DNA	DNA	YES	YES	NA	YES	DNA	DNA	YES	YES	NA
Indiana	YES	NO	*	YES	YES	NA	YES	YES	NA	YES	YES	NA
Iowa	YES	NO	15	YES	YES	NA	YES	NO	MOST	YES	YES	49
Kansas	YES	NO	DNA	YES	YES	NA	YES	NO	DNA	YES	YES	NA
Kentucky	YES	YES	NA	YES	YES	NA	YES	YES	NA	YES	YES	NA
Louisiana	YES	YES	NA	YES	YES	NA	YES	YES	NA	YES	YES	NA
Maine	YES	YES	NA	YES	YES	NA	YES	YES	NA	YES	YES	NA
Maryland	YES	YES	NA	YES	YES	NA	YES	YES	NA	YES	YES*	NA
Massachusetts	YES	NO	6	YES	NO	NO	YES	NO	6	YES	NO	NO
Michigan	YES	NO	SOME	YES	YES	NA	YES	NO	SOME	YES	YES	NA
Minnesota	YES	YES	NA	NO	NA	NA	YES	NO	48	YES	YES	NA
Mississippi	YES	YES	NA	YES	YES	NA	YES	NO	32	YES	YES	NA
Missouri	YES	NO	*	YES	YES	NA	YES	NO	MOST	YES	YES	NA
Montana	YES	NO	MOST	YES	YES	NA	YES	NO	MOST	YES	YES	NA
Nebraska	YES	NO	16	YES	NO	27	YES	NO	16	YES	NO	27
Nevada	YES	YES	NA	YES	YES	NA	YES	YES	NA	YES	YES	NA
New Hampshire	YES	NO	SOME	YES	YES	NA	YES	NO	MOST	YES	YES*	NA
New Jersey	YES	YES	NA	YES	YES	NA	YES	YES	NA	YES	YES	NA
New Mexico	YES	YES	NA	YES	YES	NA	YES	YES	NA	YES	YES	NA
New York	YES	YES*	7*	YES	YES	NA	YES	YES*	NA	NO	NA	NA
North Carolina	DNA	DNA	DNA	NO	NA	NA	YES	YES	NA	YES	YES	NA
North Dakota	YES	NO	MOST	YES	YES	NA	YES	NO	MOST	YES	YES	NA
Ohio	YES	NO	SOME	NR	NR	NR	YES	NO	SOME	NO	NA	NA
Oklahoma	YES	YES	NA	YES	YES	NA	YES	YES	NA	YES	YES	NA
Oregon	YES	NO	DNA*	YES	YES*	NA	YES	YES	NA	YES	YES	NA
Pennsylvania	YES	NO	SOME	NO	NA	NA	YES	NO	SOME	NO	NA	NA
Puerto Rico	YES	NO	SOME	NO	NA	NA	YES	NO	SOME	NO	NA	NA
Rhode Island	YES	DI	DI	YES	YES	NA	YES	DI	DI	YES	YES	NA
South Carolina	YES	NO	25	YES	YES	NA	YES	NO	25	YES	YES	NA
South Dakota	YES	NO	30	YES	YES	NA	YES	NO	30	YES	YES	NA
Tennessee	YES	NO	DNA	YES	YES	NA	YES	YES	NA	YES	YES	NA
Texas	YES	YES	NA	YES	YES	NA	YES	YES	NA	YES	YES	NA
Utah	YES	YES	NA	YES	YES	NA	YES	YES	NA	YES	YES	NA
Vermont	YES	YES	NA	YES	YES	NA	YES	YES	NA	YES	YES	NA
Virginia	YES	YES*	NA	YES	YES	NA	YES	YES*	NA	YES	YES	NA
Washington	YES	YES	NA	YES	YES	NA	YES	YES	NA	YES	YES	NA
West Virginia	YES	NO	48	YES	YES	NA	YES	NO	48	YES	YES	NA
Wisconsin	YES	YES	NA	YES	YES	NA	YES	YES	NA	YES	YES	NA
Wyoming	YES	NO	DI	YES	YES	NA	YES	NO	DI	YES	YES	NA
CANADA												
Alberta	YES	NO	DNA	YES	YES	NA	YES	DNA	NA	YES	YES	NA
British Columbia	NR	NR	NR	YES	YES	NA	YES	YES	NA	YES	YES	NA
Manitoba	YES	NO	46	YES	YES	NA	YES	NO	46	YES	YES	NA
New Brunswick	YES	NO	*	YES	YES	NA	YES	NO	*	YES	YES	NA
Newfoundland	NR	NR	NR	NR	NR	NR	NR	NR	NR	NR	NR	NR
Northwest Territory	NR	NR	NR	NR	NR	NR	NR	NR	NR	NR	NR	NR
Nova Scotia	YES	YES*	YES*	YES	YES	NA	YES	YES*	YES*	YES	YES	NA
Ontario	NO	NA	NA	NO	NA	NA	NO	NA	NA	YES	YES*	NA
Prince Edward Island	NR	NR	NR	NR	NR	NR	NR	NR	NR	NR	NR	NR
Quebec	YES	NO	MOST	YES	YES	NA	YES	NO	DNA	NO	NA	NA
Saskatchewan	YES	YES*	12	YES	YES*	12	YES	YES*	12	YES	YES*	12
Yukon Territory	NR	NR	NR	NR	NR	NR	NR	NR	NR	NR	NR	NR

LEGEND:

- * = See text for clarification
- NA = Not applicable
- NR = No response
- DI = Data incomplete
- DNA = Data not available

	32. Follow-up action to insure suspended, revoked, and cancelled licenses are returned to department/agency:
UNITED STATES	
Alabama	16 PICK-UP OFFICERS ASSIGNED TO PICK UP LICENSE
Alaska	DATE STAMP AND TICKLER FILE
Arizona	MOTOR VEHICLE ENFORCEMENT OFFICERS PICK UP LICENSE
Arkansas	INTERVIEW
California	CORRESPONDENCE ONLY
Colorado	NONE, WRITTEN NOTICE TO SURRENDER LICENSE ONLY
Connecticut	NONE
Delaware	BY MAIL
District of Columbia	LICENSE PICKED UP AT TIME OF SERVICE
Florida	BY MAIL, IF NOT SURRENDERED, PERSONAL SERVICE TO THOSE IN STATE
Georgia	IF NOT VOLUNTARILY SURRENDERED, UNIFORM MEMBER OF DPS TRIES TO GET LICENSE
Hawaii	SUSPENDED: RETAINED BY COURT; REVOKED/CANCELLED: ATTACHED TO LICENSE APPLICATION
Idaho	AUTOMATED AT ACTION TIME
Illinois	IF NOT SURRENDERED, PICKED UP BY INVESTIGATOR
Indiana	DEMAND PICKUP ORDERS AND USE ENFORCEMENT OFFICERS
Iowa	NONE AT PRESENT
Kansas	PICKUP ORDER BY HIGHWAY PATROL
Kentucky	NOTIFIED BY MAIL; IF NOT RETURNED WITHIN 30 DAYS, POLICE DEMAND ORDER
Louisiana	ORDER SUSPENDED BY MAIL; ORDER POLICE PICKUP; BLOCK DELIVERY OF LICENSE IF RENEWED
Maine	BY MAIL OR PERSONAL SERVICE
Maryland	PICKUP ORDER TO MVA INVESTIGATOR IF LICENSE NOT RETURNED
Massachusetts	LICENSE PICKUP ORDER BY ENFORCEMENT PERSONNEL
Michigan	IF NOT RETURNED BY A CERTAIN DATE, DEPT. ENFORCEMENT OFFICER PICKS OF LICENSE
Minnesota	LAW ENFORCEMENT-FINAL NOTICE
Mississippi	D.I. OFFICERS SENT OUT TO PICK UP SUSPENDED ITEMS
Missouri	NOTIFICATION & POLICE DEMAND ORDERS; STOP ACTION(COMPUTER)FOR RENEWALS & DUPLICATES
Montana	PICK UP ORDERS SERVED BY PATROLMEN
Nebraska	PICKUP ORDER TO LOCAL POLICE AND DMV LIAISON OFFICERS
Nevada	FOLLOW UP BY LAW ENFORCEMENT PERSONNEL
New Hampshire	PROPER NOTICE BY MAIL, 2nd NOTICE IS CERTIFIED MAIL, TROOPER PICK UP ORDER
New Jersey	NONE
New Mexico	NO RESPONSE
New York	POLICE ENFORCE AFTER WAITING PERIOD, LICENSES HELD IN PENDING FILES;FILE STOPPED
North Carolina	NOTIFY HIGHWAY PATROL TO PICKUP
North Dakota	BLANKET AUTHORIZATION TO ENFORCEMENT TO PICK UP AND RETURN TO OFFICE
Ohio	NO RESPONSE
Oklahoma	NO RESPONSE
Oregon	SEND POLICE A PICKUP ORDER
Pennsylvania	ISSUE PICKUP ORDER TO STATE POLICE
Puerto Rico	UPON RECEIPT OF SUSPENSION OR REVOCATION, FILED IN RECORDS & MESSAGE SENT TO COMPUTER CENTER
Rhode Island	PICK UP ORDER ISSUED TO ENFORCEMENT SECTION
South Carolina	NOTIFICATION TO HIGHWAY PATROL ENFORCEMENT
South Dakota	DEMAND ORDER ISSUED TO HIGHWAY PATROL
Tennessee	HIGHWAY PATROL PICKS UP LICENSE
Texas	DEMAND BY MAIL, IF NO RESPONSE, MAY FILE CHARGES
Utah	FOLLOWUP LETTERS AND PICKUP ORDRES TO LAW ENFORCEMENT
Vermont	NONE
Virginia	IF NOT RECEIVED WITHIN 15 DAYS, DMV REP. MAKES PERSONAL CONTACT
Washington	NONE
West Virginia	PICK UP ORDER TO STATE POLICE
Wisconsin	MAINTAIN FOLLOW - UP FILES
Wyoming	DATE DATA FILES
CANADA	
Alberta	POLICE PICK UP IF LETTER FAILS
British Columbia	CONTACT OTHER PROVINCIAL JURISDICTIONS FOR DRIVER LICENSE
Manitoba	POLICE PICKUP
New Brunswick	*
Newfoundland	NO RESPONSE
Northwest Territory	NO RESPONSE
Nova Scotia	WITHIN HALIFAX: PICKUP BY DEPT. INVESTIGATOR; OUTSIDE HALIFAX: POLICE PICKUP
Ontario	POLICE NOTIFIED
Prince Edward Island	NO RESPONSE
Quebec	IF LICENSE NOT RETURNED WITHIN 30 DAYS, FILE REFERRED TO POLICE
Saskatchewan	HIGHWAY TRAFFIC BOARD PICKS UP LICENSE
Yukon Territory	NO RESPONSE

LEGEND:
* = See text for clarification
NA = Not applicable
NR = No response
DI = Data incomplete
DNA = Data not available

	33. Driver required to appear in person for a duplicate license:	34. Time lapse (in days) between application for receipt of a duplicate license:	35. Driver record checked prior to issuing a duplicate license:	36. Issuance of a duplicate license made part of the driver's record:	37. Duplicate licenses clearly identifiable:	38. Identifiable by: a. Color code	b. Over print	c. Other	39. Notified by AAA when an International driver license issued to your state driver:	a. Made part of driver record
UNITED STATES										
Alabama	YES	0	YES	YES	YES	NO	YES	NO	NO	NA
Alaska	NO	NO	YES	YES	YES	NO	YES	NO	NO	NA
Arizona	YES	30	YES	YES	YES	NO	YES	NO	NO	NA
Arkansas	NO	20	YES	NO	NO	NA	NA	NA	YES	YES
California	YES	30	YES	YES	YES	NO	YES	NO	NO	NA
Colorado	YES	30	YES	YES	YES	NO	YES	YES*	NO.	NA
Connecticut	YES	NO	YES	YES	YES	YES	YES	NO	NR	NR
Delaware	YES	NO	YES	NO	YES	NO	YES	NO	NO	NA
District of Columbia	YES	NO	YES	YES	YES	NO	NO	YES*	NO	NA
Florida	YES	NO	YES	YES	YES	NO	YES	NO	NO	NA
Georgia	YES	30	YES	YES	YES	NO	NO	YES*	NO	NA
Hawaii	YES	45	YES	YES	NO	NA	NA	NA	NO	NA
Idaho	YES	30	YES	YES	YES	NO	YES	NO	YES	NO
Illinois	YES	0	YES	YES	YES	NO	YES	NO	NO	NA
Indiana	YES	NO	YES	YES	YES	NO	YES	NO	NO	NA
Iowa	YES	0	YES*	YES	YES	NO	NO	YES*	NO	NA
Kansas	NO	10	YES	YES	YES	NO	YES	NO	NO	NA
Kentucky	YES	0	YES*	YES	YES	NO	NO	YES*	NO	NA
Louisiana	YES	NO	YES	NO*	YES	NO	NO	YES*	NO	NA
Maine	NO	NR	YES	YES	NO	NA	NA	NA	NO	NA
Maryland	YES	20	YES	YES	YES	NO	NO	YES*	NO	NA
Massachusetts	YES	NO	YES	YES	YES	NO	YES	NO	NO	NA
Michigan	YES	30	YES	YES	NO	NA	NA	NA	NO	NA
Minnesota	NO	30	YES	YES	YES	NO	YES	NO	NO	NA
Mississippi	NO	30	YES	YES	NO	NA	NA	NA	YES	YES
Missouri	YES	*	YES	YES	NO	NA	NA	NA	NO	NA
Montana	NO	5	YES	YES	YES	NO	YES	NO	NO	NA
Nebraska	YES	NO	YES	YES	YES	NO	NO	YES*	NO	NA
Nevada	YES	0	YES	YES	YES	NA	NA	NA	NO	NA
New Hampshire	YES	21	YES	NR	NO	NA	NA	NA	NO	NA
New Jersey	NO	21	YES	NO	YES	NO	NO	YES*	NO	NA
New Mexico	YES	*	YES	NO	NO	NA	NA	NA	NO	NA
New York	NO	0	YES	YES	YES	NO	NO	YES*	NO	NA
North Carolina	YES	60*	YES	YES	YES	NO	NO	YES*	NO	NA
North Dakota	NO	*	YES	YES	YES	NO	YES	NO	NO	NA
Ohio	YES	NO	YES	YES	YES	NO	NO	YES*	NO	NA
Oklahoma	NO	NO	YES	NO	NO	NA	NA	NA	NO	NA
Oregon	YES*	NO	YES	YES	YES	NO	YES	YES*	NO	NA
Pennsylvania	NO	5	YES	YES	YES	NO	NO	YES*	DNA	DNA
Puerto Rico	NO*	5*	YES	YES	YES	NO	YES	NO	NO	NA
Rhode Island	YES	20	YES	YES	YES	NO	YES	NO	NO	NA
South Carolina	YES	30	YES	YES	NO	NA	NA	NA	NO	NA
South Dakota	YES	15	YES	YES	NO	NA	NA	NA	NO	NA
Tennessee	NO	10	YES	YES	YES	NO	YES	NO	NO	NA
Texas	YES	30	YES	YES	YES	NO	YES	NO	NO	NA
Utah	YES	21	YES	YES	YES	NO	YES	NO	NO	NA
Vermont	NO	3	YES	YES	YES	NO	YES	NO	NO	NA
Virginia	YES	NO	YES	YES	YES	NO	NO	YES*	NO	NA
Washington	YES	10*	YES	YES	NO	NA	NA	NA	NO	NA
West Virginia	NO	NR	YES	YES	YES	NO	YES	NO	NR	NR
Wisconsin	NO	14*	YES	YES	YES	NO	YES	NO	NO	NA
Wyoming	YES	45	YES	YES	YES	YES	YES	NO	YES	NO
CANADA										
Alberta	NO	90	YES	YES	YES	NO	YES	NO	YES	YES
British Columbia	YES	NO	YES	YES	NO	NA	NA	NA	NO	NA
Manitoba	YES	0	YES	YES	NO	NA	NA	NA	YES	NO
New Brunswick	NO	5	YES	YES	YES	NO	NO	YES*	NO	NA
Newfoundland	NR	NR	NR	NR	NR	NR	NR	NR	NR	NR
Northwest Territory	NR	NR	NR	NR	NR	NR	NR	NR	NR	NR
Nova Scotia	NO	NO	YES	NO*	YES	NO	NO	YES*	YES*	YES*
Ontario	NO	14	YES	YES	NO	NA	NA	NA	YES	YES
Prince Edward Island	NR	NR	NR	NR	NR	NR	NR	NR	NR	NR
Quebec	NO	10	YES	YES	YES	NO	YES	NO	NO	NA
Saskatchewan	YES	30	YES	NO	NO	NA	NA	NA	NO	NA
Yukon Territory	NR	NR	NR	NR	NR	NR	NR	NR	NR	NR

LEGEND:
- * = See text for clarification
- NA = Not applicable
- NR = No response
- DI = Data incomplete
- DNA = Data not available

	40. AAA check driver records prior to issuing an International driver license:	41. Notified by host country of violations/convictions of your state driver:	41. a. Made part of driver record and appropriate action taken	42. Forward record of conviction requiring mandatory suspension/revocation to country of visiting driver:	43. Issue identification cards:	44. Department/Agency having primary responsibility for issuing identification cards: a. Motor vehicle department/agency	b. State/local police	c. Other
UNITED STATES								
Alabama	NO	NO	NA	NO	YES	YES	NO	NO
Alaska	NO	NO	NA	NO	YES	YES	NO	NO
Arizona	NO	NO	NA	NO	YES	YES	NO	NO
Arkansas	DNA	NO	NA	YES	YES	YES	NO	NO
California	DNA	*	YES	NO	YES	YES	NO	NO
Colorado	YES	NO	NA	YES	YES	YES	NO	NO
Connecticut	NR	NR	NR	NR	NO	NA	NA	NA
Delaware	NO	NO	NA	NO	YES	YES	NO	NO
District of Columbia	YES	NO	NA	YES	YES	YES	NO	NO
Florida	NR	NR	NR	NR	YES	YES	NO	NO
Georgia	NO	NO	NA	NO	YES*	NO	YES	NO
Hawaii	NO	NO	NA	NO	YES	NO	NO	YES*
Idaho	YES	NO	NA	YES	YES	NO	NO	YES*
Illinois	NO	NO	NA	NO	YES	YES	NO	NO
Indiana	YES	NO	NA	NO	YES	YES	NO	NO
Iowa	NO	YES	YES	YES	YES	YES	NO	NO
Kansas	NO	NO	NA	NO	YES	NR	NR	NR
Kentucky	YES	NO	NA	YES	YES	NO	NO	YES*
Louisiana	NO	NO	NO*	YES	YES	YES	NO	NO
Maine	NO	NO	NA	NO	NO	NA	NA	NA
Maryland	NO	YES*	YES	YES	YES	YES	NO	NO
Massachusetts	NO	NO	NA	NO	YES*	NO	YES	NO
Michigan	*	NO	NA	YES	YES*	YES	NO	NO
Minnesota	NR	NO	NA	YES	YES	YES	NO	NO
Mississippi	YES	YES	YES	YES	NO	NA	NA	NA
Missouri	DNA	NO	NA	NO	YES	YES	NO	NO
Montana	NO	NO	NA	YES	YES	NO	YES	YES*
Nebraska	NO	NO	NA	NO	NO	NA	NA	NA
Nevada	NO	NO	NA	YES	YES	YES	NO	NO
New Hampshire	DI	*	*	YES	YES	YES	NO	NO
New Jersey	NO	NO	NA	NO	NO	NA	NA	NA
New Mexico	NO	NO	NA	YES	YES	YES	NO	NO
New York	NO	NO	NA	NO	YES	NO	YES	NO
North Carolina	NO	NO	NA	NO	YES	YES	NO	NO
North Dakota	NO	NO	NA	YES	YES	NO	NO	YES*
Ohio	NO	NO	NA	NO	NO*	YES	NO	NO
Oklahoma	NO	NO	NA	YES	YES	YES	NO	NO
Oregon	DNA	NO	NA	NO	YES	YES	NO	NO
Pennsylvania	DNA	DNA	DNA	NO	NO	NA	NA	NA
Puerto Rico	NO	NO	NA	NR	NO	NA	NA	NA
Rhode Island	DI	NO	NA	NO	YES	YES	NO	NO
South Carolina	NO	NO	NA	YES	YES	YES	NO	NO
South Dakota	NO	YES	YES	YES	YES	YES	NO	NO
Tennessee	YES	NO	NA	NO	YES	YES*	NO	NO
Texas	NO	NO	NA	NO	YES	YES	NO	NO
Utah	NO	NO	NA	YES	YES	YES	NO	NO
Vermont	NO	NO	NA	YES	NO	NA	NA	NA
Virginia	NO	NO	NA	NO	YES	YES	NO	NO
Washington	NO	NO	NA	YES	YES	YES	NO	NO
West Virginia	NR	NR	NR	NR	YES	YES	NO	NO
Wisconsin	NO	NO	NA	NO	YES	NO	NO	YES*
Wyoming	YES	NO	NA	NO	YES	YES	NO	NO
CANADA								
Alberta	YES	NO	NA	NO	NO	NA	NA	NA
British Columbia	YES	NO	NA	NO	YES	YES	NO	NO
Manitoba	NO	NO	NA	NA	NO	NA	NA	NA
New Brunswick	NO	NO	NA	NR	NO	NA	NA	NA
Newfoundland	NR	NR	NR	NR	NR	NR	NR	NR
Northwest Territory	NR	NR	NR	NR	NR	NR	NR	NR
Nova Scotia	YES*	NO	YES*	YES	YES	NO	NO	YES*
Ontario	YES	DNA	DNA	NO	NO	NA	NA	NA
Prince Edward Island	NR	NR	NR	NR	NR	NR	NR	NR
Quebec	NO	NO	NA	NR	NO	NO	NO	YES*
Saskatchewan	YES	NO	NA	NO	NO	NO	NO	YES*
Yukon Territory	NR	NR	NR	NR	NR	NR	NR	NR

LEGEND:

- * = See text for clarification
- NA = Not applicable
- NR = No response
- DI = Data incomplete
- DNA = Data not available

	45. Assign unique number to and maintain record of identification card:	a. Assign unique number only	b. Maintain record only	46. Identification card and driver license differentiated by: a. Color coded	b. Over print	c. Other	47. Eligibility for an identification card: a. Youths not eligible for a driver license	b. Adults not eligible for a driver license	c. Voluntary non-drivers	48. Identification card fee: a. Youths	b. Adults	c. Over 65 years of age
UNITED STATES												
Alabama	YES	NA	NA	NO	YES	NO	YES	NO	YES	10.00	10.00	10.00
Alaska	NO	NO	YES	NO	NO	YES*	YES	YES	YES	5.00	5.00	5.00
Arizona	YES	NA	NA	NO	NO	YES*	YES	YES	YES	5.00	5.00	5.00
Arkansas	YES	NA	NA	YES	NO	NO	NO	NO	YES	1.00	1.00	1.00
California	YES	NA	NA	NO	NO	YES*	YES	YES	YES	3.25	3.25	3.00
Colorado	YES	NA	NA	YES	YES	YES*	NA	NA	YES*	2.00	2.00	2.00*
Connecticut	NA	NA	NA	NA	NA	NA	NA	NA	NA	NA	NA	NA
Delaware	YES	NA	NA	NO	YES*	NO	*	*	*	NA	3.00	NA
District of Columbia	YES	NA	NA	NO	YES*	NO	*	*	*	3.00	3.00	NONE
Florida	YES	NA	NA	YES	NO	YES*	YES	YES	YES	3.00	3.00	3.00
Georgia	NO	YES*	NA	YES	NO	YES*	YES*	YES*	YES*	3.00	3.00	3.00
Hawaii	NA	NA	NA	NO	NO	YES*	NA	NA	NA	3.00	3.00	3.00
Idaho	NO	YES	NO	YES	NO	NO	YES*	YES	YES	5.00	5.00	5.00
Illinois	YES	NA	NA	NA	NA	NA	NA	NA	NA	NA	NA	NA
Indiana	NO	NO	YES	YES	NO	NO	NO	NO	YES	3.00	3.00	3.00
Iowa	NO	NO	YES	NO	YES	NO	YES	YES	YES	1.00	1.00	1.00
Kansas	YES	NA	NA	NO	YES	NO	YES	YES	YES	6.00	6.00	6.00
Kentucky	NO	NO	NO	NO	NO	YES*	YES	YES	YES	2.00	2.00	2.00
Louisiana	YES*	NA	NA	YES	NO	YES*	NO	YES	YES*	3.50	3.50	3.50
Maine	NA	NA	NA	NA	NA	NA	NA	NA	NA	NA	NA	NA
Maryland	YES	NA	NA	YES	NO	NO	YES	YES	YES	2.00	2.00	FREE
Massachusetts	NA	NA	NA	NA	NA	NA	NA	NA	NA	NA	NA	NA
Michigan	YES	NA	NA	NO	NO	YES*	YES	YES	YES	3.00	3.00	3.00
Minnesota	YES	NA	NA	YES	NO	YES*	YES	YES	YES	3.00	3.00	3.00
Mississippi	NA	NA	NA	NA	NA	NA	NA	NA	NA	NA	NA	NA
Missouri	NO	NO	NO	NR	NR	NR	YES	YES	YES	1.00	1.00	1.00
Montana	NO	NO	NO	NO	NO	YES*	YES	YES	YES	1.00	1.00	1.00
Nebraska	NA	NA	NA	NA	NA	NA	NA	NA	NA	NA	NA	NA
Nevada	YES	NA	NA	YES	YES	NO	YES*	YES	YES*	3.00	6.00	3.00
New Hampshire	YES	NA	NA	YES	YES	NO	NO	YES	YES	2.00	2.00	2.00
New Jersey	NA	NA	NA	NA	NA	NA	NA	NA	NA	NA	NA	NA
New Mexico	YES	NA	NA	NO	YES	NO	YES	YES	YES	NR	NR	NR
New York	NA	NA	NA	NA	NA	NA	NA	NA	NA	NA	NA	NA
North Carolina	NO	YES	NO	YES	NO	NO	NO	YES	YES*	NA	1.00	1.00
North Dakota	YES	NA	NA	NO	NO	YES*	NA	NA	NA	3.00	3.00	3.00
Ohio	NA	NA	NA	NA	NA	NA	NA	NA	NA	NA	NA	NA
Oklahoma	YES	NA	NA	NO	YES	NO	*	*	*	7.00	7.00	7.00
Oregon	YES	NA	NA	NO	YES*	NO	YES	YES	YES	5.00	5.00	5.00
Pennsylvania	NA	NA	NA	NA	NA	NA	NA	NA	NA	NA	NA	NA
Puerto Rico	NA	NA	NA	NA	NA	NA	NA	NA	NA	NA	NA	NA
Rhode Island	NO	NO	NO	NO	NO	YES*	NO	NO	YES	1.00	1.00	1.00
South Carolina	NO	YES	NO	YES	NO	NO	YES	YES	YES	2.00	2.00	2.00
South Dakota	YES	NA	NA	YES	NO	YES*	*	*	*	6.00	6.00	6.00
Tennessee	YES	NA	NA	YES	NO	NO	NO	NO	YES*	FREE	FREE	FREE
Texas	YES	NA	NA	NO	NO	YES*	YES*	YES*	YES*	5.00	5.00	5.00
Utah	NO	NO	YES	YES	NO	YES*	NO	YES*	YES*	NO	2.00	2.00
Vermont	NA	NA	NA	NA	NA	NA	NA	NA	NA	NA	NA	NA
Virginia	YES*	NA	NA	NO	NO	YES*	NO	NO	YES	NA	5.00	NA
Washington	YES	NA	NA	YES	YES	NO	YES	YES	YES	3.00	3.00	3.00
West Virginia	NO	NA	NA	YES	NO	NO	NO	YES*	YES	NA	1.00	NA
Wisconsin	YES	NA	NA	NO	YES	NA	NO	YES	YES	NA	2.00	2.00
Wyoming	YES	NO	NO	YES	YES	NO	NO	NO	YES*	NA	2.50	NA
CANADA												
Alberta	NA	NA	NA	NA	NA	NA	NA	NA	NA	NA	NA	NA
British Columbia	YES	NA	NA	NO	NO	YES*	NO	YES	YES*	NA	2.00	2.00
Manitoba	NA	NA	NA	NA	NA	NA	NA	NA	NA	NA	NA	NA
New Brunswick	NA	NA	NA	NA	NA	NA	NA	NA	NA	NA	NA	NA
Newfoundland	NR	NR	NR	NR	NR	NR	NR	NR	NR	NR	NR	NR
Northwest Territory	NR	NR	NR	NR	NR	NR	NR	NR	NR	NR	NR	NR
Nova Scotia	NA	NA	NA	NO	NO	YES*	NO	NO	YES*	NA	1.50	NA
Ontario	NA	NA	NA	NA	NA	NA	NA	NA	NA	NA	NA	NA
Prince Edward Island	NR	NR	NR	NR	NR	NR	NR	NR	NR	NR	NR	NR
Quebec	NO	NO	NO	YES	NO	NO	NO	NO	YES*	DNA	DNA	DNA
Saskatchewan	NO	NO	NO	NO	NO	NO	NO	NO	NO	NA	NA	NA
Yukon Territory	NR	NR	NR	NR	NR	NR	NR	NR	NR	NR	NR	NR

LEGEND:
- * = See text for clarification
- NA = Not applicable
- NR = No response
- DI = Data incomplete
- DNA = Data not available

APPENDIX 4

TAX DATA BY STATE

The following table is grouped by region and could prove helpful for anyone desiring to move across State lines. The ranking numbers place the States and their relative tax burdens in relationship to each other. Number 1, Washington D.C. the highest, Alabama (51) the lowest.

Per Capita Revenues From

STATE	RANK	INCOME	PROPERTY	SALES	INCOME
Connecticut	10	$ 88	$688	$425	12% above $100.000
Maine	24	227	442	273	10% above $ 50,000
Massachusetts	8	481	534	215	10% flat rate
New Hampshire	43	23	666	0	5% above $2,400
Rhode Island	13	296	561	258	10.95% above $175,000
Vermont	27	249	490	153	13.25% above $175,000
Delaware	33	587	197	0	9.7% above $40,000
Maryland	12	542	380	227	5% above $3,000
New Jersey	9	335	680	273	3.5% above $50,000
New York	2	616	650	404	13.5% above $26,000
Pennsylvania	28	301	345	229	2.2% flat rate
Wash. D.C.	1	771	638	477	11% above $25,000
Alabama	51	166	111	260	5% above $6,000
Arkansas	48	185	170	257	7% above $25,000
Florida	40	0	350	363	no tax
Georgia	30	251	285	289	6% above $10,000
Kentucky	49	232	173	303	6% above $8,000
Louisiana	44	91	166	411	6% above $50,000
Mississippi	47	100	189	333	5% above $10,000
North Carolina	37	290	229	212	7% above $10,000
South Carolona	39	241	240	242	7% above $14,000
Tennessee	50	12	213	382	6% flat rate
Virginia	29	312	343	199	5.75% above $12,000
West Virginia	31	202	191	403	13% above $120,000
Illinois	16	257	514	315	2.5% flat rate
Indiana	25	236	842	358	3% flat rate
Michigan	6	407	601	250	5.1% flat rate
Ohio	21	335	371	265	8.55% above $100,000
Wisconsin	7	458	510	288	7.9% above $40,000
Iowa	18	271	493	253	13% above $77,000
Kansas	23	233	468	248	9% above $50,000
Minnesota	4	557	466	301	14% above $32,000
Missouri	34	208	234	341	6% above $9,000
Nebraska	22	189	507	267	9.5% above $175,000
North Dakota	36	108	327	298	5.25% above $175,000
South Dakota	42	0	406	295	No tax

Colorado	14	240	445	422	8% above $14,000
Idaho	38	228	256	242	7.5% above $5,000
Montana	32	207	589	0	11% above $46,000
Utah	26	234	316	282	7.75 above $8,000
Wyoming	3	0	1,100	407	No tax
California	11	361	385	426	11% above $56,000
Nevada	35	0	298	452	No tax
Oregon	17	455	571	0	10% above $5,000
Washington	15	0	395	696	No tax
Alaska	19	2	873	117	No tax
Hawaii	5	388	278	615	11% above $61,000

APPENDIX NUMBER 5

Name Change, By State

In legal tradition, the United States attributes many of its present day laws to the original "common laws" of England. According to this system, whatever legal problems are not covered under Federal or State provisions are provided for under these laws. Since the common law of England does not specify procedures for changing one's name, it may be left to the discretion of the individual.

This is usually interpeted as the "use method. " This procedure for changing one's name has been held as valid by many courts of the land. However, some State and Federal bureaucracies being uninformed on the law, often balk at issuing legal documents using a name generated by the "use" method. They may insist on seeing an official document, signed by a State authority.

The problem for persecuted males in obtaining a legal name change via the court petition method is the possibility of centrally filed, permanent records linking the original name with the new one. This, of course, is unacceptable for those desiring absolute anonymity. However, many State's records are confined to the County or Court house where the change of name was filed. Thus, the procedure of notifying the State's Department of Vital Statistics or a central filing location is often bypassed. This would confine name change files to a very small geographical area, one which could prove most difficult for an investigator to unveil.

As a general rule, most county or probate courts maintain records on a local level only. These conditions are necessary prerequisites to maintain semi-secure privacy after a legal name change. All legal requirements should be checked out in the desired State before actually begining change of name proceedures. For complete details on name change laws, contact the Secretary of State's office in the Capitol of the State in question.

For name change information in Canada, a book titled "Changing Your Name In Canada, How To Do It Legally," by Constance Mungall, is available from International Self-Counsel Press Ltd., 306 West 25th Street, North Vancouver, B. C., Canada V7N 2G1. Last quoted price, $3.50.

Most States consider a legal name change to perpetrate fraud as a violation of law, but as an act to protect privacy by concealing one's identity is often acceptable. Eight States still do not record a known change of name on the licensee's driving record (see Appendix on drivers' licenses).

The following tables represent a very brief description of each State's procedures involved in a legal name change. Most States require a full disclosure of the original name along with other pertinent facts plus a filing fee. A lawyer is not required for a legal name change. However, there are some documents that must be filled out correctly, and a lawyer would do this for a fee.

ALABAMA

How?_______By filing a petition
Where?_____In Probate Court in County of choice
Comments:__"Use" method possible

ALASKA

How?_______By filing a petition
Where?_____Superior Court, State Capitol Building, Pouch U, Juneau, Alaska 99801
Comments:__Notice to be filed in newspaper designated by court

ARIZONA

How?_______By filing a petition
Where?_____Superior Court
Comments:__Notice by publishing

ARKANSAS

How?_______By filing petition
Where?_____Circuit Court
Comments:__list reasons for wanting name change

CALIFORNIA

How?_______By filing petition
Where?_____Superior Court
Comments:__Notice by publication, "Use Method" recognized, four week waiting period

COLORADO

How?_______By filing petition
Where?_____Superior, District or County Court
District Court of Colorado
145 U.S. Court House
Denver CO 80202
Comments:__Notice by publication

CONNECTICUT

How?_______By filing petition
Where?_____Superior Court, Deputy Court Administrator
Superior Court, Drawer D, Station A, Hartford
Connecticut 06106
Comments:__a lawyer may be required

DELAWARE

How?_______By filing petition
Where?_____District Court
Comments:__notice by publication

WASHINGTON. D.C.

How?_______By filing petition
Where?_____U.S. District Court
Comments:__Notice by publication, must be resident

FLORIDA

How?_______By filing petition
Where?_____Circuit Court
Comments:__Must be resident, answer detailed questions about personal history

GEORGIA

How?_______By filing petition
Where?_____Superior Court
Comments:__Answer detailed personal questions concerning personal history

HAWAII

How?_______By filing out a petition and a Decree
Where?_____Lieutenant Governers office
Comments:__Extremely detailed filing system, lawyer recommended

IDAHO

How?_______No known existing laws
Where?_____No information
Comments:__Contact Secretary of State's Office. "Use" method should prevail

ILLINOIS

How?_______By filing a petition
Where?_____Circuit Court
Comments:__Resident for six months. Detailed personal information required

INDIANA

How?_______No known existing laws
Where?_____No information
Comments:__"Use" method should prevail

IOWA

How?_______By filing petition
Where?_____District Court
Comments:__Detailed personal history required. Must be resident

Kansas

How?_______By filing petition
Where?_____District Court
Commentsy: Publication. Must be resident. Detailed personal history required

KENTUCKY

How?_______Petition not required
Where?_____Local County Court
Comments:__Local records only

LOUISIANA

How?_______Name change forms
Where?_____District Court
Comments:__Need lawyer. "Use" method void

MAINE

How?_______By filing petition
Where?_____Probate Court
Comments:__Lawyer needed

MARYLAND

How?_______By filing petition
Where?_____Circuit Court
Comments:__Lawyer not required

MASSACHUSETTS

How?_______By filing petition
Where?_____Probate Court
Comments:__Notice by publication

MICHIGAN

How?_______By filing a petition
Where?_____Probate Court
Comments:__Detailed personal history required

MINNESOTA

How?_______By filing petition
Where?_____District Court
Comments:__Must provide two personal witnesses

MISSISSIPPI

How?_______No laws at present
Where?_____None specified
Comments:__"Use" method should be valid

MISSOURI

How?_______By filing petition
Where?_____Circuit Court
Comments:__20 day waiting period, file by publication

MONTANA

How?_______By filing petition
Where?_____District Court
Comments:__File notice by publication, local records only

NEBRASKA

How?_______By filing petition
Where?_____District Court
Comments:__Must be resident one year, notification by publication

NEVADA

How?_______By filing petition
Where?_____District Court
Comments:__Notification by publication

NEW HAMPSHIRE

How?_______No known laws
Where?_____Probate Court
Comments:__"Use" method should apply

NEW JERSEY

How?_______No known laws, no forms
Where?_____County Court
Comments__local records only

NEW YORK

How?_______By filing petition
Where?_____Depending on place of application. Civil or local Courts
Comments:__Past history of applicant required

NORTH CAROLINA

How?_______By filing petition
Where?_____Superior Court
Comments:__Must provide character witnesses and numerous de tails of past history

NORTH DAKOTA

How?_______By filing petition
Where?_____District Court
Comments:__Six months' residency required. Notification by publication

OHIO

How?_______By filing petition
Where?_____Probate Court
Comments:__One year residency required. Notification by pub lication

OKLAHOMA

How?_______By filing petition
Where?_____District Court
Comments:__Very restrictive proceedure

OREGON

How?_______By filing a petition
Where?_____Circuit Court
Comments:__Notification by publication. Must give reasons to Judge

PENNSYLVANIA

How?_______By filing a petition
Where?_____In Probate Court
Comments:__"Use" method not recognized. Many details requir-ed

RHODE ISLAND

How?_______By filing petition
Where?_____Probate Court
Comments:__Lawyer may be required

SOUTH CAROLINA

How?_______By filing a petition
Where?_____Circuit Court
Comments:__"Use" method is questionable, investigate

SOUTH DAKOTA

How?_______By filing a petition
Where?_____Circuit Court
Comments:__Resident for six months, notification by publica tion, other details about personal history

TENNESSEE

How?_______Filing an application
Where?_____Probate or County Courts
Comments:__"Use" method may be acceptable. Local records only

TEXAS

How?_______Filing an application
Where?_____District Court
Comments:__Local records only

UTAH

How?_______By filing petition
Where?_____District Court
Comments:__One year residency required. Notification by publication

VERMONT

How?_______By filing petition
Where?_____Probate Court
Comments:__Detailed personal history required. Notification by publication

VIRGINIA

How?_______By filing a petition
Where?_____Circuit Court
Comments:__Detailed personal history required

WASHINGTON

How?_______By filing a petition
Where?_____Superior Court
Comments:__Local records only

WEST VIRGINIA

How?_______By filing an application
Where?_____Circuit Court
Comments:__One year residency required. Local records only

WISCONSIN

How?_______By filing an application
Where?_____County Court
Comments:__Local records only. Must be resident

WYOMING

How?_______By filing a petition
Where?_____District Court
Comments:__Must be resident for two years

ORDER FORM

PLEASE SEND ME MY OWN PERSONAL COPY
OF JASON ROBERT'S "HOW TO LOSE YOUR EX-WIFE (FINANCIALLY) FOREVER".

SHIP TO:

NAME ______________________________
(PRINT)

ADDRESS ______________________________
(PRINT)

CITY ______________ STATE ______________ ZIP ________

COPIES ________ @ $17.95 EA. PLUS SHIPPING SEE RATES BELOW TOTAL ________

UTAH RESIDENTS ADD $1.00 PER COPY SALES TAX ________

CREDIT CARD ORDERS ONLY!
1-800-247-6553
OPERATORS ON DUTY AROUND THE CLOCK!

MasterCard VISA DISCOVER

Each book $17.95 plus shipping. See rates below.

SHIPPING ________

AMOUNT ENCLOSED

SEND ORDER FORM WITH MONEY ORDER OR CHECK TO:

LIBERTY BELL PRESS AND PUBLISHING CO.
SUITE 3-183
4700 SOUTH 900 EAST
SALT LAKE CITY, UTAH 84117

SHIPPING OPTIONS

4TH CLASS, ADD $2.00 PER BOOK (2–3 WEEKS)
1ST CLASS, ADD $4.00 PER BOOK
OVERNIGHT, ADD $15.00 PER BOOK

RATES APPLY IN CONTINENTAL USA ONLY